JAMES FORTEN

Liberty's Black Champion

JULIE WINCH

Adapted from

Julie Winch,
A Gentleman of Color:
The Life of James Forten

© Julie Winch, 2011. All rights reserved.

No portion of this book may be reproduced or used in any form,
or by any means, without prior written permission by the publisher.

First printed January 2011

Printed in the United States of America

ISBN 978-0-9832069-0-3

Portrait of James Forten
(Leon Gardiner Collection, Historical Society of Pennsylvania)

Contents

Acknowledgments v

Sources and Citations – A Note vi

The Forten Family Tree vii

James Forten – Timeline viii

Introduction – An End and a Beginning 13

Chapter 1 – Inheriting Liberty 15

Chapter 2 – Sail-loft and Schoolroom 21

Chapter 3 – Liberty for All? 31

Chapter 4 – "I Never Will Prove a Traitor" 41

Chapter 5 – Venturing to England 51

Chapter 6 – Mastering His Trade 58

Chapter 7 – South Wharves 67

Chapter 8 – A Talent for Making Money 75

Chapter 9 – Raising a Family in Freedom 80

Chapter 10 – A Community Takes Shape 91

Chapter 11 – "A Man of Colour" Speaks Out 106

Chapter 12 – Captain Cuffe's Plan 118

Chapter 13 – "America is Our True Home" 129

Chapter 14 – Allies in Liberty's Cause 137

Chapter 15 – A Family Commitment 151

Chapter 16 – Law-Breakers and Lawmakers 161

Chapter 17 – Keeping Hope Alive 170

Chapter 18 – An Honest Man 176

Afterword – Sweet Freedom's Song 187

Sources and Citations 190

Selected Resources 203

Acknowledgments

My students at the University of Massachusetts Boston helped me with this project in many ways. They encouraged me, challenged me, and provided me with technical assistance.

Robert Goodwin, my graduate research assistant, and his wife, Julie Kiernan, put their computer skills to work and constructed the Forten family tree.

The following students in my Freshman United States History survey course read each one of the chapters and gave me insightful and invaluable feedback:

James Bennette	Rebecca LaPierre
Victoria Chamberlain	Olamide Oladosu
Melvin F. Clark Jr.	Miko Rin
Luis Diaz	Brianna Savard
Eduardo Franco	Wallace Washington
Darshan Gandhi	William P. Whittington
Lori Gordon	Ilda Zenelaj
Dana Lamb	

Four of my fellow historians, Dee Andrews, Roy Finkenbine, James O. Horton, and James Brewer Stewart, took time out of their busy schedules to review the manuscript, and my husband, Louis S. Cohen, helped in innumerable ways.

My thanks to each and every one of you. Telling James Forten's story truly has been a collaborative endeavor!

Sources and Citations

Rather than overload the text of *Liberty's Black Champion* with citations, I have tried to strike a balance between supplying too much information and too little. Readers will see that I identify at the end of the book the source of each and every quotation, unless the source is very obvious.

For those who want to know more, I have included a short list of useful books and articles, along with links to websites. Those who want to know even more should refer to my full-length biography of James Forten, *A Gentleman of Color* (New York, 2002).

Nineteenth-century newspapers provided me with a wealth of information for *A Gentleman of Color* and for *Liberty's Black Champion*. More and more newspapers are being digitized and made searchable on-line. I hope readers will use the links I have included to look at some of those newspapers. While I would not discourage anyone from sitting in an archive and leafing through a newspaper page by page, digitization not only preserves fragile newsprint but makes it possible to accomplish in minutes what once took hours.

The Forten Family Tree

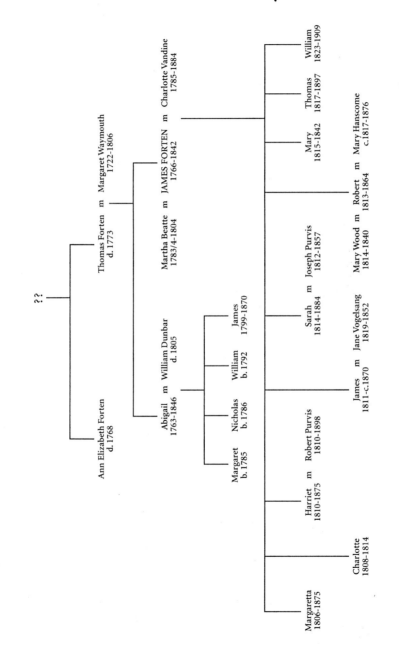

James Forten – Timeline

1680s	JF's great-grandfather arrives in Pennsylvania from West Africa as a slave
1700-1720	JF's grandfather gains his freedom. JF's father, Thomas Forten, is born free
1721/22	Birth of Margaret Waymouth, JF's mother
1763	Birth of JF's sister, Abigail
1766	**Birth of JF (September 2)**
1773	Death of Thomas Forten
1773-75	JF attends Friends' African School
1781	JF goes to sea as a privateer and is captured by the British
1782	JF returns to Philadelphia
1784	Abigail Forten, JF's sister, marries William Dunbar. Dunbar and JF sail to England
1785	JF returns from England and begins an apprenticeship with Robert Bridges
1792	Robert Bridges buys 50 Shippen Street for JF
1798	JF takes over Robert Bridges's sail-loft
1803	JF marries Martha (Patty) Beatte
1804	Death of Martha Beatte Forten. Death of William Dunbar
1805	JF marries Charlotte Vandine

1806	Death of Margaret (Waymouth) Forten JF purchases 92 Lombard Street as family home Birth of 1st child, Margaretta Forten
1808	Birth of 2nd child, Charlotte Forten
1810	Birth of 3rd child, Harriet Davy Forten
1811	Birth of 4th child, James Forten Jr.
1813	Birth of 5th child, Robert Bridges Forten JF authors *Letters from a Man of Colour*
1814	Death of daughter, Charlotte, age 6 Birth of 6th child, Sarah Louisa Forten
1815	Birth of 7th child, Mary Isabella Forten
1816-17	American Colonization Society formed. JF moves from support to vocal opposition
1817	Birth of 8th child, Thomas Willing Francis Forten
1823	Birth of 9th child, William Deas Forten
1831	JF helps fund publication of the *Liberator* Marriage of Harriet Davy Forten and Robert Purvis
1836	Marriage of Robert B. Forten and Mary Virginia Wood
1838	Marriage of Sarah Louisa Forten and Joseph Purvis
1839	Marriage of James Forten Jr. and Jane M. Vogelsang
1840	Death of grandson, Gerrit Smith Forten, and daughter-in-law, Mary Wood Forten
1842	**Death of JF (March 4)**

An End and a Beginning

The Englishman was puzzled. Sir Charles Lyell had been in Philadelphia long enough to know what most white people in the city thought of their black neighbors. And yet, here he was, standing on the sidewalk on a Sunday morning in early March of 1842, witnessing a remarkable display of respect for a black man. He stood and watched as the funeral procession set off from a prosperous-looking home on Third and Lombard Streets, in the heart of the city. He could see the dead man's family—his widow, his children, their spouses, and a bunch of grandchildren. Their mourning clothes were elegant. They had money *and* good taste. Behind the family walked several dozen servants and employees. Clearly the deceased had been wealthy.

What really caused Sir Charles to stare, though, was the sight of hundreds of people, black and white, rich, poor, and "middling," following along behind the hearse. Several thousand more were doing what he was doing—standing and watching. And well-to-do white men were actually removing their hats. A few were even bowing as the casket passed by. But who was it that they were honoring? Lyell found himself burning with curiosity.

When he asked his friends, they told him that the dead man's name was James Forten. They explained that he had been one of the leading sailmakers in the city, and that was why so many captains and ship-owners had turned out for the funeral. James Forten had been well-known in the business community. He had lived in Philadelphia virtually all his life, he had a reputation for honesty, and he had been well-liked. That thumbnail sketch was good enough for Sir Charles. He made a note of the curious event in his travel memoir and turned his attention to other matters.

Sir Charles Lyell's curiosity was easily satisfied; but, if we allow ours to be, we ignore the life of a truly remarkable man. To understand who James Forten was, the tumultuous times he lived through, and just what he contributed to his community and to the nation he held dear, we have to delve much deeper. He was everything Sir Charles's friends said he was, but he was much more besides. To begin to have a sense of the true meaning of his life we have to go back...beyond *his* lifetime to the lives of his ancestors, who came to America not as free people seeing before them a land of opportunity, but as "cargo" in the holds of slave-ships. The mission of James Forten, the descendant of men and women who knew only slavery and oppression, was to remake America as a land of liberty for every one of its people. This is his story. It is also a forgotten piece of this nation's story.

CHAPTER ONE

Inheriting Liberty

When James Forten was born on September 2, 1766, in a modest home on Third and Walnut Streets, in the part of Philadelphia known as Dock Ward, no one outside his immediate family took note of the event. And yet the birth was significant, not just because of who James Forten would become but because of what he represented. He belonged to the fourth generation of his family to live in British North America and the third to be born in Pennsylvania. As a grown man he liked to boast that his family had lived in Pennsylvania since the days of the colony's Quaker founder, William Penn. However, when they looked at him, what most white Philadelphians saw was not a member of an old and deservedly proud family, but an "African."

In a sense, James Forten *was* an African. That was the term whites applied to anyone with any visible trace of African ancestry. It was also how black men and women often described themselves. "African" he might be, but James Forten's world was not the world his great-grandfather had known when he arrived in Philadelphia from West Africa as a slave in the 1680s. James's ancestor was not

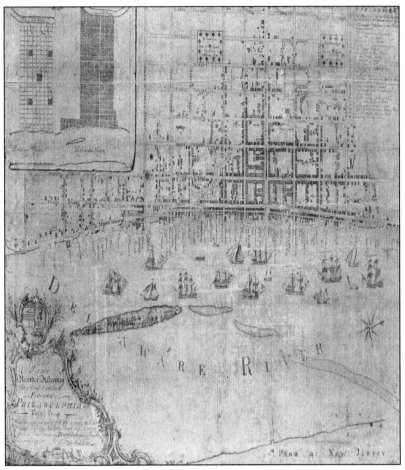

Nicholas Scull, *Plan of Philadelphia in 1762*
(Library Company of Philadelphia)

This shows the city that James Forten would have known as a child.

the only African in William Penn's fledgling colony. Dutch and Swedish pioneers who had farmed and traded along the Delaware for half a century before the creation of Pennsylvania owned African slaves. As for William Penn, although he was at first uneasy about slavery, he accepted it as a necessary evil. His Quaker colonists followed his lead, often without his initial misgivings.

Most slaves came into Philadelphia in groups of a dozen or so because slave traders generally preferred to sell their human cargo in the West Indies, where prices were higher. Even so, the population of enslaved Pennsylvanians grew steadily. By 1700 there were over two hundred in Philadelphia, and more in the surrounding countryside. Among that first generation of black Philadelphians was James Forten's great-grandfather. We do not know his name, but we can deduce a few things about him. He was physically strong, or he would not have survived the horrors of the slave ship or his first winter in Pennsylvania. He was quick to master new skills. Slave-owners in Philadelphia expected their slaves to be able to perform a wide range of tasks. They also required them to learn English and become at least nominally Christian.

As for the enslaved, there is plenty of evidence that black people in and around Philadelphia were struggling to forge a sense of community. As early as 1693, masters complained about "tumultuous gatherings of the negroes" on the Sabbath, as black Philadelphians took the opportunity to socialize away from the watchful eyes of their owners. Perhaps James Forten's great-grandfather slipped away now and again to join in those "tumultuous gatherings." We know so little of his life—not the name his parents gave him, his slave name, the name of his owner, or how many times he was sold. What we *do* know is that he took an enslaved woman as his wife. In virtually every colony in British North America children inherited the condition of their mother. Had James Forten's great-grandmother been white or Indian, her child would have been free. James Forten always said, though, that he knew his grandfather, his father's father, had been born a slave, and that meant both of his great-grandparents had been slaves.

James Forten's great-grandparents spent their lives in slavery, but their son became free, although how he managed that Forten never explained, telling a friend simply: "My grandfather obtained his own freedom." Perhaps his grandfather earned enough to buy his liberty, or perhaps he was freed by one of those rare individuals who became convinced that slavery was a sin.

Becoming free was no easy matter, and neither was remaining free. In colonial Pennsylvania free black people could not vote, marry white people, travel where they wished, trade in certain goods, consume alcohol, mingle with slaves, be idle, disobedient, or in short do anything that disturbed the white community. The penalty was a whipping and, for most offenses, re-enslavement. By a mix of luck and determination, James Forten's grandfather stayed free and, just as important, found a free woman to marry. Their children were born into freedom.

Facts about the lives of James Forten's parents are hardly more plentiful than they are about his grandparents and great-grand-parents. James's father was Thomas Forten, and he was freeborn. His mother was Margaret Waymouth, and she may have been born a slave. Margaret was 41 in 1763 when her daughter, Abigail, was born and 44 when she gave birth to James. Why was she so much older than most women in colonial Philadelphia when she had her first child? Quite possibly because she was not free until she was well into her thirties. If she was a slave, she knew that any child she bore would be a slave. She and Thomas may have delayed their marriage and chosen not to begin a family until they had secured her freedom.

We know more about Thomas than we do about Margaret. He had been born in the same neighborhood as his son, and at some point he had learned to read and write—a remarkable achievement for any laboring man, black or white, in 18th-century Philadelphia. Thomas probably had kinfolk in and around the city, but the only person we know for sure was related to him was Ann Elizabeth Forten. She was his sister.

Young James grew up with no recollection of his aunt, since she died before his second birthday, but her presence was real enough. Ann Elizabeth had property to leave and, because she was childless, she left it all to James's sister, Abigail. How had Ann Elizabeth acquired the nice furniture, jewelry, and elegant silk gowns that featured in her will? In a setting where women, let alone unmarried black women, had few opportunities in life, all the indications are that at some point Ann Elizabeth Forten had had a wealthy white lover. She had made the best of her situation, and it was little Abigail who benefitted. That Ann Elizabeth had one item of "property" she did not leave to her niece also says a lot about the complex situation of people of color in colonial Philadelphia. Ann Elizabeth was a slave-owner. She freed her West Indian bondwoman Jane in her will, but she had made use of Jane's unpaid labor for years.

Ann Elizabeth left her estate to white Quaker teacher Anthony Benezet, a fervent opponent of slavery and a friend to many in the black community. He would hold the property in trust for Abigail. When Abigail was old enough to marry, her inheritance would provide her with a decent dowry; and that would get her a good husband. Ann Elizabeth reasoned that her nephew did not need her money. James was a boy. He would learn his father's trade and make his own way in the world. And Thomas Forten did have a skilled trade to pass on to his son. In a time and a place where most black people were held as slaves, and where almost all of those who were free were forced into back-breaking menial labor, Thomas was a skilled craftsman, and he would teach his trade to his son. That, along with his freedom, would be James Forten's inheritance.

CHAPTER TWO

Sail-Loft and Schoolroom

Thomas Forten was a sailmaker. As a young man, he had found work in one of the city's many sail-lofts, and that was probably how he met his future employer, Robert Bridges. An "African" without capital or connections, Thomas was not in a position to secure a formal apprenticeship and truly master every aspect of the sailmaker's trade. Robert Bridges was more fortunate. He had money. He could get an apprenticeship and eventually open his own loft. When he had his own loft, he hired Thomas.

It was one of the realities of life in colonial Philadelphia that Thomas Forten, a free black man, found himself working for pay alongside slaves and white bound laborers who earned nothing at all. As he became more prosperous, Robert Bridges purchased Irish indentured servants for set terms of years and black slaves for life. However, he obviously did not see Thomas Forten as being on the same level as his unfree workers. Even though Thomas had never served an apprenticeship, he had picked up many of the skills needed to be a competent sailmaker, and Bridges paid him a decent wage. When Thomas asked if he could bring his son to the loft to learn the basics of the trade, Bridges raised no objections. A bright lad should be encouraged, and he was happy to have James around.

For James Forten in his early years, the sail-loft was his playroom and his schoolroom. Like other sailmakers, Robert Bridges conducted his business on the upper floor of a warehouse. Sailmakers needed ample room for marking out the plans for each sail and laying down the canvas. It was only the upper story of a building that could provide floor space free from the obstruction of supporting posts.

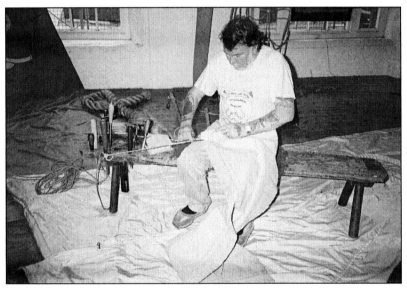

Sailmaker at work
Sewing canvas sails by hand has changed very little from the 1700s to today.

Of course, sails and canvas could not be brought up narrow staircases, so most lofts had a block and tackle to hoist sails up the side of the building. Another sailmaker recalled being entertained in his boyhood, as no doubt James was, by unexpected visitors. When vessels came into port from the West Indies, spare canvas that had been stored in the sail-lockers was shaken out to reveal enormous cockroaches, which dropped onto the loft floor and just *had* to be chased.

The workday began early in the loft, as it did in virtually every workshop in the city. Thomas Forten and the other men checked in with Bridges, stowed away their food for the day, and changed from their street clothes into their canvas work outfits, for Bridges wanted no dirt on his expensive sail-cloth. James probably started out sweeping the floor, with his father impressing on him the importance of keeping it clean, since it was where the canvas would be laid down and cut.

From pushing a broom James graduated to picking over "shakings," the pieces of canvas and cordage left over as sails were cut and shaped. An odd corner of canvas could be used as a patch, and rope could be picked apart and made into oakum for caulking. A child's nimble fingers and sharp eyes made him valuable for this kind of recycling work.

Another task involved even more responsibility. In an iron kettle James would make up a mixture of turpentine, tallow, and beeswax, while always being careful not to let it boil over. Once it cooled a little, he would shape it into small blocks. His father and the other sailmakers would run their sewing thread through the wax to waterproof it and make it easier to work with. Again James needed a keen eye. Wax flakes around the benches had to be picked up—scraped up with an old knife, if necessary—and put back into the kettle. Nothing went to waste.

As he grew stronger, James could be assigned one of the least pleasant tasks around the loft—rubbing pungent Stockholm tar into the hanks of sewing twine. It made your arms ache and your hands stink for days, but it had to be done. The tar protected the twine from mildew and prolonged the life of the finished sail. A much more appealing task, and one generally classed as "boy's work," was holding up the canvas as Robert Bridges or his foreman cut it to size. This gave a would-be apprentice the chance to see exactly how sails were designed.

Thomas gradually introduced James to the tools of his trade. As soon as his fingers could grasp a needle, he was taught to sew. Sailmaker's needles were much larger than those his mother and sister used to make and repair his clothes. There were many different types of needles. As he became more familiar with his work environment, James learned to distinguish among them according to their size, shape, and function. Thomas stressed the need to keep these expensive precision tools in good repair, sharpening them on a water stone, greasing them with lard before he began sewing, and then cleaning them with polishing rouge before storing them in a leather or canvas case.

Once he had stuck himself a time or two, James came to understand that as vital a part of the sailmaker's gear as his needles was his palm—a strip of leather shaped to encircle the hand, leaving the fingers free. There was a hole for the thumb, and a metal disc or "eye" at the heel of the hand. The trick was to push the needle through the canvas with the "eye," using the palm like a large thimble.

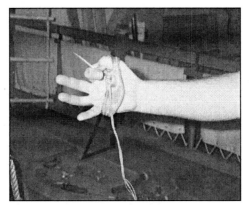

Palm and needle
The first tools young James would have learned to use.

The main item of furniture in the loft was the sailmaker's bench. It provided both a seat and a work surface, while keeping all the tools a craftsman needed close at hand. On one end was a sail-hook to which the sailmaker fastened his canvas so he could keep it pulled tight across his knees while he sewed.

There were slots in the bench for storing fids, the large tapered pins for opening up the strands in lengths of rope ready for splicing. Each had to be stored in its appropriate place in the bench, within reach but clear of the floor. Fids were expensive, and it was essential that their points did not become blunt and damage the canvas or cordage the sailmaker worked with.

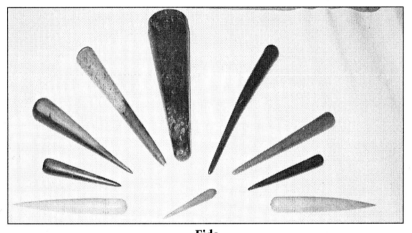

Fids

Fids of different sizes were basic tools, and James Forten would have learned to use them.

Apart from the fids, there was a whole array of marlin spikes, stabbers, and awls, as well as mallets ranging in size from the huge "commander" to the much smaller variety. James learned their names from his father and his workmates. He also learned the different types of stitching, and the weight and feel of every grade of canvas and cordage. That knowledge, mastered in his childhood, would serve him well in the years to come.

More tools of the sailmaking trade.

While he was working for Robert Bridges, Thomas Forten began branching out on his own, taking on small commissions that
did not require much space or equipment. He worked hard and
met with some success. Thomas did not use his earnings to buy
real estate. Like most of Philadelphia's laboring people, he did not
own the home in which he and his family lived. Instead he invested
his spare cash in loans at interest, some with a Quaker carpenter,
Israel Hallowell, and some with an Irish-born teacher, James Cannon.

Thomas Forten's relationship with James Cannon was an intriguing one. Cannon had arrived in Philadelphia in 1766. He had
a degree from Scotland's Edinburgh University, and he began teaching classes in reading, writing, arithmetic, navigation, surveying,
algebra, and geography. He eventually became Professor of Mathematics at the College of Philadelphia (today's University of Pennsylvania). He owned a slave, but that was just a sad fact of life in

Philadelphia. Cannon and his wife interacted with Thomas and Margaret and their children on a friendly basis. They were neighbors, and they may also have gone to church together each Sunday since both of the families were Anglicans. Just possibly it was James Cannon who taught Thomas Forten, his friend and neighbor, to read and write.

In 1773 tragedy struck the Forten family. Thomas died. He may have succumbed to a lingering ailment or he may have come down with a sudden illness. Margaret and the children were lucky that whatever killed him did not kill them. In small, cramped homes it was difficult to avoid contagion.

Margaret did what she had to. She called in the loans her husband had made to Cannon and Hallowell because she needed the cash, and she probably asked Anthony Benezet for an advance on Abigail's legacy from her aunt. She also sought Benezet's advice about James. She wanted to send her son to school. Now that his father was dead, his practical training in the sail-loft was over, at least for a while. What he would do with his life Margaret did not know, but she did know that his opportunities would be vastly improved if he could read and write. However, she was illiterate, so she could not teach him. Benezet put her in touch with the trustees of the Friends' African School.

The African School was an institution close to Benezet's heart, and it is easy to see why. Eager to challenge the notion that black people were intellectually inferior to whites, he had begun a night school at his home for adults and children around 1750. By 1770 his efforts had attracted the attention of his fellow Quakers. At long last they were discussing abolishing slavery, and to prepare their slaves for freedom they decided to open a school. They would admit enslaved children whose owners were willing to let them attend, and they would admit free black children.

Anthony Benezet teaching African-American children
From J.W. Barber, *Historical, Poetical and Pictorial American Scenes* (1850)
James Forten always spoke fondly of his friend and mentor.

Although he did not run the African School, Benezet helped shape its curriculum, and his *Pennsylvania Spelling Book* was a classroom staple, as it was in many white schools. Benezet watched over the school and filled in from time to time, but James Forten's teacher was actually Jacob Lehre. Like Benezet, Lehre combined piety with years of classroom experience, and he was liked and respected by his pupils. James thrived at the African School. All too soon, though, he had to leave. By the spring of 1775 his mother and sister could not afford to keep him at school any longer. They needed him to go out to work and help them pay the rent and put food on the table. Anthony Benezet helped James find a job. Robert Bridges may have hired him from time to time, but the economy was in crisis; and anyway James was too young and as yet too inexperienced to do much around the sail-loft. He went to work for a local store-keeper, cleaning his shop and doing some clerking. It wasn't what Margaret had hoped her son would do, but it was the best work he could get for now, as events spiraled out of control and Britain's thirteen colonies, Pennsylvania among them, headed towards open conflict with the mother country.

The momentum had been building for a decade. The year before James Forten was born, Parliament passed the Stamp Act. Before his first birthday the hated Townshend Duties received royal approval; and colonists responded by refusing to buy British goods. Before James turned four, Crispus Attucks and his companions had been killed in the Boston Massacre.

He was seven when the Boston Tea Party occurred. On May 19, 1774—a year before his much more famous ride through the Massachusetts countryside to alert the Minute Men that the Redcoats were on their way to Lexington Green—Paul Revere rode into Philadelphia with an urgent appeal for help from the people of Boston. Britain had retaliated for the destruction of the tea by passing the Coercive Acts, a sharp reminder to Bostonians of their duty to obey their king. Two weeks later the British closed the port of Boston until the tea was paid for. On June 1, the day the Boston Port Act went into effect, many Philadelphia merchants closed their stores as a sign of sympathy. Church bells were muffled as if for a funeral. Ships in the harbor flew their colors at half-staff. Three days later, on the king's birthday, there were none of the usual celebrations. Philadelphia was a city in mourning.

Young though he was, James Forten realized something was going on. There were mobs in the streets, heated discussions on street corners, and a growing sense of tension. The first Continental Congress met at Carpenters' Hall, just yards from his home, in September 1774. He and his family saw the delegates arriving. What all this activity might lead to neither they nor their white neighbors knew. However, they felt the rising tide of anger. If that anger boiled over into armed rebellion, and if Britain sent in troops to restore order, they could hardly escape being caught up in the resulting turmoil.

By the time he celebrated his ninth birthday, James Forten was aware, if only dimly, of the contradictions in his young life. He was free in a city where many hundreds of black people were enslaved. He was literate at a time and in a place where few of his social standing could read or write. He had the elements of a skilled trade, but he might never be able to graduate to doing anything beyond sweeping floors and stacking shelves. Although he was descended from one of the first people to settle in Philadelphia, he knew that his great-grandfather had arrived in chains. James Forten was an "African" and a British subject. Soon he would have to decide whether to assume another identity and declare himself to be both an "African" and an "American."

~

CHAPTER THREE

Liberty for All?

By the spring of 1775 most Philadelphians sensed that something was in the air. James Forten was no exception. An inquisitive child, he ranged about the city in his free time, pausing to watch ship traffic on the Delaware, picking up scraps of information, and glancing at any newspapers, pamphlets or handbills that came his way. He knew from what he read that white colonists were speaking of themselves as "slaves" of the British. Did that mean they were questioning whether it was right to hold black people in bondage? Some thought they should question that. Forten's friend Anthony Benezet, for instance, denounced slaveholding Patriots as hypocrites. How could they urge war in the name of freedom while denying freedom to others? And on the very eve of war, Benezet and a group of other white Philadelphians who felt as he did established the Society for the Relief of Free Negroes Unlawfully Held in Bondage (later known as the Pennsylvania Abolition Society). As the crisis deepened, the likes of Thomas Paine and Dr. Benjamin Rush argued that slavery was immoral and linked its abolition to the success of the Patriot cause. Of course, the Fortens were free, but the existence of slavery put their freedom in jeopardy. They could easily be seized and sold as alleged runaways.

With the clashes outside Boston in April 1775, the meeting of the second Continental Congress a few blocks from his home the following month, and the mustering of troops in the city, James Forten knew his world was changing. In the short term, he saw that events hundreds of miles away could have an economic impact close to home. Congress announced a trade embargo in response to the fighting in New England. There would be no imports from Britain to the thirteen colonies and no exports from those colonies to Britain. Philadelphia merchants might support the Patriot cause, but not all of them were ready to sacrifice their profits. There was a mad dash to get ships ready to sail ahead of the embargo. Perhaps there was casual work for James in Robert Bridges's sail-loft, even if it was just fetching and carrying and doing simple sewing tasks, as ships were hastily fitted out and last-minute repairs made to their sails and rigging.

As the war escalated, startling news reached Philadelphia. In Virginia the British governor had done the unthinkable. While George Washington and the other Patriot commanders wrangled over arming even free black men, let alone slaves, Lord Dunmore had offered freedom to the slaves of Patriot masters if they volunteered to fight for the king. The response was overwhelming. Slaves in Virginia fled in droves, and word spread far beyond Virginia that the British intended to liberate all the slaves in America. Slaveowners were shocked to the core, and slaves were ecstatic. In Philadelphia rumors were rife of unruly slaves defying whites and telling them they would be sorry when Dunmore and his black troops turned up. In the end, no rebellion occurred. The rumors *were* only rumors. Most of Philadelphia's slaves preferred to see how the war went and who made them the most attractive offer for their loyalty. Their goal was physical freedom, but for people like the Fortens who were already free, the choices were more complex.

On July 8, 1776, nine-year-old James Forten, alerted by the unexpected noonday ringing of the church bells, elbowed his way into
the crowd gathering in the State House Yard and heard the Declaration of Independence read to the public for the first time just
four days after the Continental Congress formally approved the
break with Britain. He remembered that lifelong. What he heard,
of course, was not Jefferson's original version, with its stern condemnation of the slave trade, but a document carefully phrased to
unite the delegates from the various colonies. Yet, for all of its shortcomings, it sounded inspiring that humid summer day.

Within months, though, it seemed the high-sounding phrases
of the Declaration counted for nothing against the military might
of Great Britain. General Washington suffered one defeat after another. The members of the Continental Congress fled Philadelphia,
as did many ordinary civilians, amid reports that the British were
advancing on the city. Martial law was imposed; and, to make things
worse, smallpox and camp fever broke out among the troops stationed in the city. Hundreds died. (losing in battle, supplies & men)

Citizens of a Loyalist persuasion, and many of the enslaved,
awaited the arrival of the British with keen anticipation, while the
Patriots argued about how best to defend Philadelphia. Panic subsided with Washington's victories at Trenton and Princeton, but
this was only a respite. When the spring thaw came in 1777, the
authorities set to work constructing defenses along the Delaware—
Fort Mercer, Billingsport, and Fort Mifflin. Additional protection
was provided by the *chevaux de frise*, rows of iron-tipped spikes
designed to hole any vessel that ran onto them. A fleet of small
armed vessels and fire-ships was held in readiness.

Just how badly the Patriot cause was faring became painfully
obvious toward the end of the summer of 1777. In a show of force
Washington paraded his troops through Philadelphia. They hardly
had the look of a conquering army. To begin with, they had no

uniforms. Each man was dressed in his everyday clothes, with a sprig of green in his hat as an emblem of hope. Like uniforms, weapons, and food, hope was in short supply as the Patriots marched off to fight the British. Did James Forten watch the parade, scanning the ranks to try to spot black or brown faces? They were there to be seen. The general who in 1775 had been so reluctant to enlist Americans of African descent, even if they could prove they were legally free, had changed his tune. He needed recruits, and he was so desperate that he did not care about the color of their skin. If they were willing to serve, that was good enough.

Washington planned to halt the British on the Brandywine Creek. The roar of cannon could be heard in Philadelphia throughout the evening of September 11, and the next day news of the battle's outcome reached the city. The British had won. British troops under General Sir Henry Clinton marched into Philadelphia a few days later. Their first priority was to clear the rebel defenses along the Delaware. The Patriot forces at Billingsport fled after setting fire to the fort, while the tiny Patriot fleet sailed upriver to a safer spot under the guns at Fort Mercer and Fort Mifflin. As for the *chevaux de frise*, the Patriots' secret weapon, the British simply dredged it up and took it to pieces.

A last-ditch effort by Washington to drive the British forces under General Howe out of Germantown ended in failure on October 4. Howe followed Clinton into Philadelphia and gave the order to make the assault on the remaining rebel strongholds along the Delaware. The attack on Fort Mercer proved costly. The commander of the Hessians (German mercenaries in the pay of the British) was killed, along with three hundred of his men, and two British warships were lost. After that the British concentrated on Fort Mifflin, firing upon it until it was a smoking ruin.

Eleven-year-old James Forten heard the great guns booming and smelled the acrid smoke of a British warship or a Patriot fort ablaze downriver. He knew black men had played a part in the defense of Fort Mercer because he had watched them march out of the city to garrison the fort and he had heard talk in the street that they had acquitted themselves well. But now they and their white comrades-in-arms had gone to join Washington in winter quarters at Valley Forge. As 1777 drew to a close, the British were firmly in control of Philadelphia.

Once the winter set in and the river froze, there were shortages of food and fuel. When spring arrived and the ice on the Delaware melted, supplies came in again, but that did not really help, since greedy merchants intercepted farmers bringing goods to town, bought up their produce, and resold it at inflated prices. The struggle to feed her children taxed Margaret Forten's energy and ingenuity more than it had done at any time since the death of her husband and the family's descent into poverty.

Eventually the British abandoned Philadelphia to focus their attention elsewhere. About one-third of the citizens had stayed through the occupation, some because they were Loyalists, but many, like the Fortens, because they had nowhere else to go. The British army marched out on June 18, 1778, and the British fleet left the following day, taking as many as three thousand civilians to the Loyalist stronghold of New York City. With them went a good number of black men and women, most of them the slaves of Patriots who had left them behind when they fled ahead of the British assault on Philadelphia the previous year.

Even as the war dragged on, James Forten knew another war was being fought. Pennsylvania's lawmakers were debating the future of slavery. In March 1780 they passed an abolition law. It wasn't perfect by any means. It freed only the children of slaves, and not until they turned 28. As for people of African descent who were already free, it did not say they were now citizens. Still, the first steps had been taken. And the new law explicitly linked abolition and independence. Lawmakers expressed their joy "that it is in our power to extend a portion of that freedom to others, which hath been extended to us," adding, "It is not for us to inquire, why, in the creation of mankind, the inhabitants of the several parts of the earth were distinguished by a difference in…complexion. It is sufficient to know that all are the work of an Almighty Hand."

James Forten realized that many people of color in Pennsylvania had not waited for lawmakers to act. They had made the Revolutionary War a war for personal freedom. They had fled from their masters, petitioned the courts to declare their enslavement unjust, or thrown in their lot with one side or the other in the contest for control of British North America. What the quality of citizenship might be for a black Patriot he would have to wait and see, but the abolition law, with its statements about justice and an end to prejudice, won him over. He became a Patriot. As he grew older and stronger, he resolved not merely to identify as a Patriot but to fight as a Patriot.

The restoration of Patriot control brought new wealth to Philadelphia as it emerged as a major privateering port. Growing up in a port city, James Forten knew a lot about privateering. The commissioning of privateers was a practice used by the British and the French in practically every naval conflict they engaged in. Now it was the turn of the Patriots. The owner of a merchant ship would look for a captain who was aggressive and ready to take a risk. Then he would secure "letters of marque"—in essence a license from the authorities to attack enemy shipping—and get the vessel ready to sail. She would need to be armed for war and she would require a far larger crew than she carried in peacetime. Once out at sea, the privateer would attack any enemy trading vessel she encountered. When a vessel was captured and brought into port, she and her cargo would be "condemned" (legally judged to be a prize of war) and auctioned off. The authorities took their share and the owner his. The rest was divided among the members of the crew according to their rank. The system of shares was worked out beforehand, and everyone knew exactly what he would be entitled to. Even the humblest powder-boy could expect to make a good amount of money if a cruise went well and many prizes were taken.

In his wanderings down by the Delaware James Forten paused to watch as ships' carpenters overhauled merchant vessels, strengthening decks to bear the weight of cannon. Other vessels were being purpose-built as commerce-raiders. It seemed anyone with money to invest wanted a stake in a privateering cruise. Robert Bridges, for instance, owned or part-owned six vessels. Quite possibly James picked up casual work from him and his partners as the vessels were fitted out or repaired.

With each day that passed, James Forten's desire grew to serve the country and the cause he had come to regard as his own, to see more than the streets of his native city, and to make money. Nothing else would satisfy him than to become a privateer. A tall, athletic fourteen-year-old—the year was now 1781—eager to serve, and blessed with some knowledge of how to repair sails, he was unlikely to be rejected by any captain because of the color of his skin. Most cared about one thing only—an individual's willingness to serve.

Stephen Decatur, the captain James Forten hoped to sign on with, had compiled an impressive list of victories. In the summer of 1781 he took command of merchant Francis Gurney's new vessel, the 450-ton, 22-gun *Royal Louis,* named for America's ally, King Louis XVI of France. For a ship of that size Decatur needed to recruit a large crew so that, as he took one prize after another, he could assign enough men to sail each vessel into port without risking the prisoners regaining control of the vessel or seriously under-manning his own ship.

James Forten had chosen his captain. It now only remained for him to persuade his mother to let him go to sea. Margaret was understandably reluctant to part—perhaps forever—with her only son, but he nagged her constantly and she finally gave in. After an emotional farewell, James Forten, three months short of his fifteenth birthday, left home for the first time. Classed as a "boy," since he was under 16, he was entitled to a tiny one-half of a full share of the spoils, but a successful cruise could net him a good amount of prize money—and Captain Decatur had a reputation as a "lucky" captain.

On board the *Royal Louis* the fact that he was black hardly set James Forten apart. A tenth of the crew of two hundred was black. If anything set him apart it was that he was literate and could sign his name to the ship's articles. However, he was not an experienced sailor, so he could only be assigned to work where he was supervised by older and more knowledgeable hands. Going aloft to reef or let out the lighter sails, working at the capstan to raise or lower the anchor, swabbing decks, and working in the galley were all tasks likely to fall to his lot. In the event of a battle, he would stay on the gun-deck to fetch powder and shot from the shot-locker, and generally keep out of the way of the gun crews.

The first cruise of the *Royal Louis* was a great success. Decatur had instructions from Gurney to sail between the British-held ports of New York and Charleston, South Carolina. The *Royal Louis* captured five vessels quickly and easily. Their captains took one look at the well-armed privateer bearing down on them and either surrendered without firing a shot or offered only token resistance. However, a sixth opponent, the *Active,* did not give up quietly. She was smaller than the *Royal Louis* and carried fewer guns, but her captain chose to fight. Eventually, though, he was obliged to strike his colors. The *Active* was brought into port by a prize-crew from the *Royal Louis* "amid the loud huzzas and acclamations of the crowd that assembled upon the occasion." The vessel was valuable,

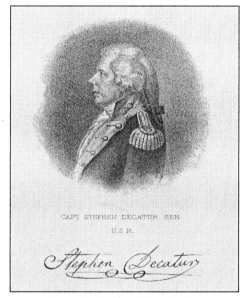

CAPT STEPHEN DECATUR, SEN.
U.S.N.

Captain Stephen Decatur Sr.
(Gratz Collection, Historical Society of Pennsylvania)
James Forten always spoke proudly of serving with Decatur.

but her "cargo" was even more valuable. Her captain was carrying Royal Navy battle-plans. That was why he had fought back. He had been trying desperately to save the documents entrusted to him.

There was no doubt about it. James Forten's first cruise had been a great success. He had returned unscathed and with money in his pocket, and he could take pride in having served his country by helping to capture a vessel carrying vitally important dispatches. His recollection of the "loud huzzas" of the crowd on the wharves as the *Active* was brought into port suggests he had been a member of the prize-crew and had shared in that moment of triumph.

As he prepared for his second cruise, events were moving quickly, thanks in part to the loss of the dispatches aboard the *Active*. Back in the early summer, the British naval commander in New York City, Admiral Graves, had heard reports that a large French naval force was poised to sail from Saint Domingue (modern-day Haiti) to join up with the French fleet at Newport, Rhode Island. Together they would provide General Washington with naval support for an attack on New York. Graves had sent the *Active* to find the British fleet in the West Indies and request assistance. The reply—that Admiral Hood was aware of the danger, that he would sail to New York, and that he would look in on the Chesapeake Bay en route to see if the French fleet was menacing Lord Cornwallis's army in Virginia—was being carried aboard the *Active*.

The British fleet was on its way from the West Indies, but Graves did not know that. A duplicate set of dispatches finally reached him, but many weeks after the ones that had been seized by Decatur and his crew. For quite some time Graves did not know what was happening. Meanwhile, Cornwallis had allowed his army to become trapped on Virginia's Yorktown peninsula. He was awaiting a rescue by sea that never came. Abandoning plans to take New York, Washington hurried south to cut off any retreat by land. On September 2 he marched his troops through Philadelphia. James Forten spent his fifteenth birthday watching the day-long parade. Fifty years later he wrote: "I well remember that when the New England Regiments passed through this city…there was [sic] several Companies of Coloured People, as brave Men as ever fought." This did indeed seem to be a war that knew no lines of race. A few weeks later, buoyed up with patriotism, desire for adventure, and thoughts of more prize money, he made his way back to the *Royal Louis*.

CHAPTER FOUR

"I Never Will Prove a Traitor"

By the time James Forten set sail on his second cruise on October 7, 1781, the siege at Yorktown was well under way. The British fleet coming from the Caribbean had not spotted the French fleet in the Chesapeake for the simple reason that the French had been delayed by bad weather. Admiral Hood assumed the French were ahead of him on their way to New York and that Cornwallis's army was in no danger. Reassured, he sailed on. The French ships arrived five days later and Cornwallis was trapped. Hood reached New York, realized what had happened, and spurred Graves into action, but it was too late. In the Battle of the Chesapeake the British tried unsuccessfully to dislodge the French and reach Cornwallis. Eventually a dispirited Graves set sail for New York to prepare another rescue mission. The sea lanes to the south of the Delaware were swarming with British and French vessels, merchantmen and warships. It was the luck of the draw whether the *Royal Louis* would encounter a lightly-armed trading vessel or a heavily-armed ship of the line.

Captain Decatur had heard before he left port that there were a couple of British frigates cruising off the Capes of Virginia, but he had a strategy worked out. The *Royal Louis* was part of a small fleet of cruisers and merchantmen sailing out of Philadelphia. Decatur and the other captains anchored upriver and waited for the wind to change. If the British were lying in wait at the mouth of the Delaware, a northwesterly wind would force them out to sea. If they were simply heading back to New York, they would find it no easy matter to turn and pursue a dozen or more vessels making for the south with the wind behind them. The first part of the plan worked. The wind changed and under cover of night the Americans sailed down the Delaware and into the open sea. It seemed the gamble had paid off—until the dawn revealed two British warships uncomfortably near.

At first light on October 8 a lookout on *HMS La Nymphe* spotted three vessels to the northwest—two brigs and a ship. The master of *La Nymphe* signaled John Bazely of *HMS Amphion*, and Captain Bazely responded. *La Nymphe* would go after the brigs while he pursued the much larger ship.

The *Royal Louis* tried to outrun the *Amphion*, James Forten and his crewmates desperately following Decatur's orders to hoist more sail. But if Decatur was an experienced captain so was his opponent. John Bazely had entered the Royal Navy in his early teens and had worked his way up the ranks by his skill and ingenuity. He was no novice in the art of seamanship.

Gaining quickly on his quarry, Bazely identified her as an American privateer. As he had suspected, she was fair game. Still, he was willing to try to see if he could fool her captain into thinking the *Amphion* was a friendly vessel. He ordered his men to hoist French colors. Decatur did not fall for that trick. He knew a British warship when he saw one. He fired on the *Amphion,* and the chase continued. By noon the vessels were only half a mile apart. An hour later, off the Virginia coast, the *Amphion* moved in for the kill. Bazely opened fire, and Decatur, knowing he was outgunned, surrendered.

Exhausted, the crew of the privateer awaited their fate. Bazely sent over a prize-crew to take charge of the *Royal Louis.* Then he lowered boats to ferry the Americans over to the *Amphion.* Meanwhile, *La Nymphe* had also had good hunting. When she rendezvoused with the *Amphion* she had the two brigs in tow. It was dusk by this time, too late to safely do much shifting about of prisoners. The next day, though, Bazely transferred some of his captives to *La Nymphe.* He could not accommodate and feed all two hundred of the privateer's crew. Once the transfer had been completed, the two British warships and their prizes charted a course for New York.

Captain John Bazely, Esq.
He captured James Forten; then he and his son befriended
James and offered him a home in England.

Confined below decks on the *Amphion,* James Forten feared the worst. He had heard that the British enslaved their black prisoners. Was that to be his fate? In fact, a very different future awaited him. Captain Bazely had his two sons on board the *Amphion.* John Jr.

was a midshipman, and this was his second or third cruise, but Henry was proving something of a problem. He was twelve, and this was his first cruise. Entered on the muster as his father's servant, he had few duties assigned him, and he was bored. He needed someone to keep him out of trouble, but Captain Bazely could not spare any member of his crew. Then he happened to notice a tall, dark-skinned youth among his prisoners. Struck by James Forten's "honest and open countenance," Bazely singled him out and ordered him to watch over Henry.

Over the next day or two the forced association between James Forten and Henry Bazely deepened into a friendship in an unusual manner. They both delighted in playing marbles. Henry was awed by his companion's skill, and in an odd moment he drew his father's attention to it. The captain was suitably impressed, but what impressed him more than James Forten's dexterity was the bond that was forming between his son and the young prisoner.

Just before noon on October 12, four days after the capture of the *Royal Louis*, the *Amphion* and *La Nymphe* parted company. *La Nymphe* would take her prisoners and all of the prize vessels to New York while the *Amphion* hunted down more prizes. Forten and the other prisoners would stay on board until the *Amphion* finished her patrol.

More prizes came the way of the *Amphion*, and more prisoners joined the men from the *Royal Louis*. Then, on the afternoon of October 16, the *Amphion* encountered a large convoy from Britain making for New York. The convoy, so Captain Bazely learned, was on its way to rendezvous with Admiral Graves for another bid to rescue Cornwallis and his army. The *Amphion* joined the convoy, occasionally firing signal guns to tell straggling vessels to fall in to their stations. On the morning of the 19th the convoy met up with Graves's fleet. It must have been an impressive and, at the same time, a rather fearsome sight to James Forten and his fellow Americans—the full might of the Royal Navy readying for an attack. What they could not know, any more than Bazely or Graves, was that it was too late. Cornwallis had already surrendered.

The *Amphion* sailed south with Graves's fleet as it got underway. Then, with the lighthouse at Sandy Hook in sight, she left the fleet and began working her way up to New York. On October 22 she fell in with *La Nymphe*, which had discharged her prisoners a week earlier. A pilot was sent over, and by noon the following day the *Amphion* was moored in the East River. Her master recorded in his log that towards evening on the 23rd his crew was "Employ'd Carr[y]ing our Prisoners to the Prison Ship." James Forten was entered on the muster of the prison-hulk *Jersey* as prisoner #4102.

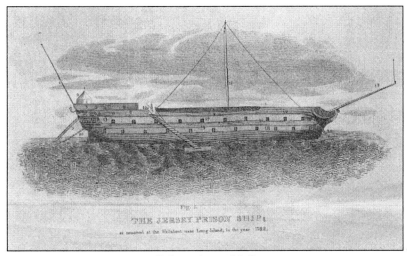

"The Prison Ship"
From Thomas Dring, *Recollections of the Jersey Prison Ship* (1829)
Historical Society of Pennsylvania

Had he chosen, James Forten need never have set foot on the *Jersey*. As the *Amphion* neared New York, Captain Bazely sent for him. He approved of the growing friendship between his son and the young Philadelphian, and he had a proposal to put to James.

The captain offered to send him to England with Henry. There was no suggestion that the Bazelys meant to compel James to go with them. The choice was his. The family would pay for his education and see to it that he had a good career ahead of him, especially since they had influence in the Navy and could make the right connections for him. He had only to say the word. To Bazely's utter astonishment, James Forten rejected the offer, insisting: "I have been taken prisoner for the liberties of my country, and never will prove a traitor to her interest."

A deeply disappointed Captain Bazely did what he could for his prisoner, keeping him on board until the last possible moment in case he changed his mind, and finally writing a letter to the commander of the prison-ship requesting that he be treated decently. James Forten never forgot Bazely's kindness or the incident that had attracted the captain's attention in the first place. In later life he would often speak of that fateful game of marbles on the *Amphion's* deck and speculate that it had probably saved him from enslavement on a sugar plantation in the West Indies.

In the short term, though, James Forten's position was little better than that of a slave. His chances of getting off the prison-ship alive were not good. When she had sailed out of the Plymouth Dockyard in England, the *Jersey* had been a fine-looking vessel, but that was back in 1736. Her glory days long over, she was now a prison-hulk, without sails, rigging, masts or rudder. She had no need of them because she would never again sail the oceans of the world. She was anchored in Wallabout Bay in New York's East River as a floating warehouse for American captives.

As he was rowed across to the *Jersey*, James Forten was no doubt appalled by the stench coming from the ship. After clambering up the side of the hulk, he was searched for weapons but allowed to keep his clothes and bedding. His name was entered on the list for exchanges. If he survived long enough, freedom would come when

his name reached the top of the list and there were British prisoners available to be traded for Americans.

His first priority was to get himself accepted into the basic social unit on the *Jersey*, the mess. A mess consisted of six men, and a
new prisoner had to seek out a mess where a member had recently
been exchanged or had died. The men from the *Royal Louis* who
had been held aboard *La Nymphe* had already been on the *Jersey*
for over a week. Forten and the contingent from the *Amphion* were
shipmates, and they welcomed the new arrivals without question.
James Forten had no problem finding a place in one of the messes.
Once they had accepted Forten, the "old hands," who knew the rou-
tine of the ship, would help him find his way about. They would
also become his most loyal friends. Mess-mates were, to all intents
and purposes, brothers.

James Forten's first night on the *Jersey* was far worse than his
first night on the *Amphion*. Even with limited resources, Captain
Bazely had done his best for his prisoners, but conditions aboard
the prison-hulk were truly deplorable. As he tried to sleep—kept
awake by hunger, for he had missed the day's hand-out of rations,
and by the groans and delirious ravings of his fellow captives—he
surely questioned his wisdom in rejecting Bazely's offer of a comfortable life in England.

Morning meant the chance to escape the noise and foul smells
below decks, look around, learn more about the floating prison
and her inhabitants—and eat. Every day at nine o'clock a member
of each mess collected the men's food ration from the steward. The
ration consisted of bread, meat, peas, and oatmeal, and the quality
was dreadful. One captive wrote of pounding the bread on the deck
to dislodge the worms. Another recalled that the *Jersey's* officers
kept hogs penned up on the gun-deck, and the starving prisoners
would steal the bran from their trough.

The members of the mess handed over their food allowance to

the cook to be cooked in a huge copper kettle divided in two. The rations for each mess were distinguished by a string "tally" and the food was deemed cooked when the cook said it was! He boiled the peas and oatmeal in fresh water, and the beef in fetid sea water. To try to avoid food poisoning, the men in each mess would hoard fresh water from their daily ration and try to persuade the cook to let them hang their own small kettle over the fire, separate from the vast boiler.

Was there any way to escape from the *Jersey*? James Forten asked his mess-mates. Yes, they told him, one could agree to enlist in the Royal Navy, but hardly anyone chose that route. What about making a break for freedom? That was virtually impossible, they explained. Assuming you could get over the side of the prison-hulk undetected, you faced a two-mile swim, a barrier of mud-flats, and the knowledge that Long Island was under British control. If you made it ashore, the locals would hand you back.

Undeterred, James Forten put his mind to work and came up with a plan. An American officer was to be exchanged for a British officer, and Forten asked if he could hide in the man's sea-chest. At the last moment, though, he gave up his chance of freedom to Daniel Brewton, a white Philadelphian two years his junior, who was in worse shape than he was. Forten actually helped lower the chest of "old clothes" into the waiting long-boat. Brewton made it home and never forgot that act of kindness. He and James Forten became lifelong friends.

James Forten had no illusions about what he was giving up by letting Brewton escape in his place. A poor diet, inadequate clothing, and overcrowding took their toll on even the healthiest captives. Some went mad. Others died of disease. Fleas, ticks, and lice infested the ship's occupants. The *Jersey* was an ideal breeding-ground for that scourge of the eighteenth century, smallpox. Some prisoners performed crude inoculations on themselves, using pus from the sores of those already infected. Many others succumbed.

Every day there were deaths on board. If the dead man had a blanket, his friends were allowed to sew him up in it. The burial party would then strap him to a board and lower him over the side into a small boat. They rowed ashore under armed guard, dug a trench, and laid his body in it, along with the bodies of all those who had died the previous night. The graves were so shallow and so close to the shoreline that bodies were often washed out to sea during a storm.

The days dragged on for James Forten and his fellow captives. While the surrender at Yorktown had left the Patriots with thousands of British prisoners on their hands, negotiations for exchanges were painfully slow. Then, out of the blue, in the seventh month of his captivity, Forten was ordered up on deck. He and a bunch of other prisoners were told to get their belongings. Their turn to go home had finally come.

Margaret Forten had given up her son for dead. The young man who came home to her was very different from the boy who had sailed out of port so many months before. After his release from the *Jersey,* he had walked barefoot from New York to Trenton, New Jersey, where the townspeople had taken pity on him and given him shoes and food. Despite the kindness of the citizens of Trenton, James Forten reached home in a wretchedly bad condition—painfully thin, and practically bald as a result of scurvy.

Back in Philadelphia recuperating from his ordeal, how did James Forten interpret what the Revolution meant for him? Crammed into a dark, stinking hold, poorly fed, and with men around him dying of disease and neglect every day, he knew the suffering endured by his great-grandfather on his voyage into slavery a century before. But when all was said and done, James Forten was not a slave in his months on the *Jersey.* Nor was he shunned by his fellows because of the color of his skin. The prisoners banded together for mutual support and survival. With his fellow Americans on the *Jersey,* and most obviously with his mess-mates, he shared a sense of brotherhood so deep that he would give up his chance of freedom to one of them, and that individual would respond with a lifetime of friendship.

In later years James Forten would draw on his wartime service to argue that he deserved the same rights as other Americans. But the dreams of lasting brotherhood soon faded. If he needed proof, it came, ironically enough, on Independence Day. In 1776 the nine-year-old James Forten had stood in the crowd in the State House Yard to hear the Declaration of Independence read to the people for the first time. Decades later the adult James Forten and his children had to stay home on July Fourth or face the threat of violence if they ventured into the streets to join in the celebrations. What, he was left wondering, had happened to the promises of freedom and equality? What was the true meaning of the independence that he and countless other black Patriots had fought to win for their country?

CHAPTER FIVE

Venturing to England

With his painful trek back to Philadelphia the war came to an end for James Forten. The care and affection his mother and sister lavished on him, decent food, rest, and his own robust constitution combined to repair the ravages of sickness and malnutrition. His recovery *had* to be a speedy one. Money was as scarce as ever in the Forten household. He was soon back at work, most likely sewing canvas in Robert Bridges's sail-loft.

The next major event for the Forten family was Abigail's wedding. The records reveal nothing about William Dunbar other than that he was a sailor and he was legally free by the time he and Abigail wed. The ceremony took place at St. Paul's Episcopal Church on April 10, 1784. There was little time to celebrate. William had already signed on for a voyage to London aboard Captain Thomas Truxtun's ship, the *Commerce,* and he had persuaded his new brother-in-law to sail with him.

As a privateer during the war, the *Commerce* had carried fourteen guns and a crew of fifty. Now that the war was over, the crew of fifty had shrunk to two dozen and the heavy guns were gone from the deck. As for Truxtun, the one-time privateering captain was now a merchant with a store to stock and customers eager to buy imported British goods. He made one voyage after another to London while his partner managed their store. He was always in need of a good crew, and such matters as race were far outweighed by considerations of skill and reliability.

James Forten and William Dunbar said their goodbyes and prepared to ship out. The *Commerce* left Philadelphia on April 21 and sailed downriver to New Castle, Delaware to pick up a few passengers. Once out of the Delaware River, she bore north, past Long Island Sound. Icebergs and fogs off the Grand Banks obliged Truxtun to chart a more southerly course than he would have done had he been making the crossing in August or September. Later in the season he might have headed as far north as Newfoundland, but at this time of year it was wiser to keep to the south of Nantucket.

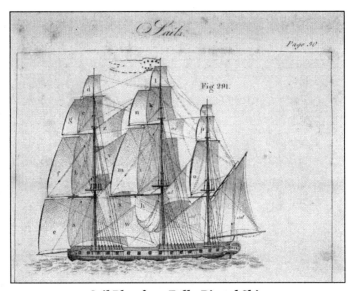

Sail Plan for a Fully-Rigged Ship
From Darcy Lever, *The Young Sea-Officer's Sheet Anchor* (1819)
(Library Company of Philadelphia)

Once out into the Atlantic, the *Commerce* sailed on for days without sight of land. Because she was making for London rather than Liverpool, she kept well to the south of Ireland. The first land her lookout spotted was the Scilly Isles, off the coast of Cornwall. Soon Truxtun and his crew were working their way through the southwestern approaches to England. As they maneuvered through the busy Straits of Dover, Truxtun never left the helm; and Forten, Dunbar, and the rest of the men were constantly employed trimming sails, taking soundings, and watching the movements of other vessels. The *Commerce* sailed east and then north into the Thames Estuary. This stretch of water was a challenge in the art of seamanship even for someone of Truxtun's expertise, but the *Commerce* continued on her way without incident, eventually tying up at one of the wharves just below London Bridge and within sight of the Tower.

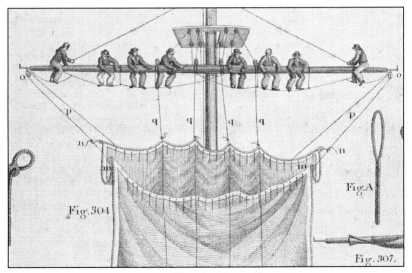

Bending the Foresail
From Lever, *The Young Sea-Officer's Sheet Anchor*
James Forten would have known all about this difficult and dangerous task, and he probably went aloft during his times at sea.

This, then, was the great metropolis James Forten could have visited as the Bazelys' protégé. Now here he was, a seventeen-year-old sailor on an American vessel and knowing no one in London. And yet, for some reason, he decided to take his chances and stay, at least for a while. William Dunbar was not about to linger. He would want to hurry back to Abigail, and with a steady fellow like Dunbar now a member of the family, Forten need feel no anxiety about his sister and mother. Why should he not stay and see what London had to offer?

The *Commerce* did not leave for Philadelphia directly from London. She sailed from the port of Deal, a dozen or so miles from Dover, where the Bazelys lived. It is tempting to imagine James leaving London on board the *Commerce*, helping maneuver her down the Thames, being put ashore with the pilot as she made ready to sail, watching her until she was just a dot on the horizon, and then taking the coast road to Dover to turn up on the Bazelys' doorstep. It is a nice picture, but there is not a scrap of evidence to suggest that he ever met the Bazelys again after he left the *Amphion* in Wallabout Bay. Most likely he stayed behind in London. Someone who could sew canvas quickly and neatly would not be long without work. In a score of yards great and small downriver from the Tower of London vessels of various sizes were under construction, from huge East Indiamen to modest fishing wherries. James Forten knew from gossip on the wharves and in the riverside taverns, as well as from his own observations, that the London yards were facing a shortage of skilled workers. Why not stay when there was the prospect of good wages and valuable work experience?

What did James Forten make of the great city in which he had been set adrift at his own request? Although he was city-bred, nothing could prepare him for London. Philadelphia, which had been the largest city in the British Empire after London, was home to some 50,000 people. London's population was ten or twelve times that. Philadelphia was not even a hundred years old when James Forten was born. London's history went back to Roman times. As for the physical environment, Philadelphia was so much cleaner. The London of 1784 was a filthy, congested metropolis. It was summertime when James Forten arrived, and the city stank in the heat. The Thames was an open sewer running through its heart. As winter approached, the stench was masked by coal smoke. A dingy yellow-gray pall hung over the city for days at a time and irritated the lungs and the eyes of those not used to it.

The part of London James Forten became most familiar with lay south of the Thames and east of the Tower. Neighborhoods like Wapping and Limehouse, Shadwell, Stepney, Rotherhithe, Poplar and Blackwall were close to the wharves and shipyards, and they were where sailors from around the globe congregated. Life was tough here. Work was hard and poverty never far away. It was here, though, among the rope-walks and the warehouses, the ship chandleries and the sail-lofts, that James Forten found employment and companionship.

In the dockside communities, as in most of the rest of London, his complexion did not mark him out as an oddity. There had long been a black presence in the city. Planters visiting from the West Indies often brought their personal attendants with them, and some of those slaves, to the annoyance of their masters, made their escape, often with the aid of white friends.

In 1772, when Lord Mansfield handed down his verdict in the *Somerset* case—a verdict that did not free every slave in Britain, as is often assumed, but did prevent the forced removal of slaves from the country—there were between 15,000 and 20,000 black people in England. Many lived in London, and there were sizable black enclaves along the river and in areas like Paddington and Mile End. On the south bank of the Thames, where he lived and worked, James Forten would have rubbed shoulders with Africans and West Indians, black Britishers, and black Americans like himself.

In the poorer quarters of London blacks and whites lived in a harmony born of shared poverty and desperation. Black men far outnumbered black women, and as a result they often married or lived with English women, especially those in domestic service like themselves. Like most of the laboring poor, black Londoners, whether native-born or newcomers, faced a daily struggle to survive, even at the best of times.

When James Forten arrived in England, attitudes towards black people were undergoing a crucial shift. London was full of American Loyalists. Clinging together in exile, they seemed to do nothing but complain—about the food, the weather, and most of all about the compensation they had received from the British government. If the white Loyalists got at best a lukewarm welcome, their black counterparts were most definitely not wanted. Despite the ties of friendship and intermarriage that existed among some blacks and whites in England, there had always been an undercurrent of racism, and the influx of black refugees caused it to intensify, at least among those in positions of power.

Perhaps as many as a thousand black Loyalists had been evacuated to Britain at the end of the War of Independence. Although there were success stories, by and large the refugees did not prosper. What was to be done with them? Could they somehow be removed from the country? Perhaps the Sierra Leone project was already being talked about while James Forten was in Britain. However, plans for the West African colony did not really begin to crystallize until after he returned home to Philadelphia.

And what of the abolition cause that would eventually consume so much of his energy? When James Forten arrived in London, the crusade was only just beginning. British Quakers led the movement, but they were aided in their endeavors by popular revulsion over the news of the treatment of the captives aboard the British slave-ship the *Zong*, whose captain had deliberately drowned 131 slaves to collect the insurance money. A host of spiritual and cultural concerns, from respect for "traditional" English freedoms to the desire to help the less fortunate, to romantic notions about the "noble savage," were fusing together into an antislavery campaign. However, freeing slaves in Britain's far-flung empire was one thing. Extending the rights of Englishmen to black people in Britain was another matter entirely.

CHAPTER SIX

Mastering His Trade

Why did James Forten decide to return to Philadelphia in 1785? Perhaps the shifting racial climate made London a less attractive place than it had seemed at first glance. Perhaps he had felt out of place as a black American who was not a Loyalist but an ardent supporter of American independence. Or perhaps his year abroad had been simply the result of a young man's desire to see the world before settling down. Whatever the reason for his decision, getting back to Philadelphia posed few problems. He needed only to ask around in the taverns and on the docks to find out which masters wanted to take on an extra crew member.

He came home to find he had a baby niece, Margaret. The following year Abigail and William had another child, Nicholas. Other developments were less joyful. James Forten's mentor and friend, Anthony Benezet, was dead. He had died soon after Forten's departure for England, and his simple Quaker funeral had been attended by many members of the black community whose lives he had touched.

Once he was home, James Forten soon found work. He apprenticed himself to Robert Bridges. The arrangement suited the needs of both men. Bridges had known James Forten since James had come to work with his father as a child. Bridges had almost certainly hired him over the years. He knew him to be a good worker, and he appreciated the younger man's eagerness truly to master the sailmaker's craft.

When James Forten began his apprenticeship, Robert and his wife Jemima had seven children. An eighth would be born in 1788. In the normal course of events, Forten would have completed his apprenticeship, graduated to being a journeyman, and remained a journeyman as Culpepper Bridges and his brothers came of age and assumed control of their father's business. Even if his sons pursued other careers, Robert Bridges had daughters who would surely marry and bring him sons-in-law to learn the trade and eventually take over the sail-loft. In fact, though, prospects were brighter for James Forten than might have been supposed.

So much about James Forten's future was rooted in Robert Bridges's past. Bridges had become a sailmaker because his father, Edward, a successful merchant, had died when Robert was a child, and his guardians had used some of his inheritance money to bind him out to learn a trade. He had prospered. In 1785, at age 46, he had a thriving business and a nice home, as well as hundreds of acres of undeveloped land in the western counties of Pennsylvania. In social terms, however, he had not fared as well as he would have if his father had lived and if the mercantile firm of Edward Bridges & Co. had survived to become Edward Bridges & Son. Robert Bridges wanted his children to do better than he had. He expected his sons to become merchants or doctors or lawyers, not sailmakers. As for his daughters, he did not want them to marry tradesmen. He wanted them to "marry up" socially. James Forten was well aware of Robert Bridges's plans for his children. With his potential competitors out of the running because they were destined for other things, a hard-working and ambitious young man in the Bridges sail-loft could justifiably look to the day when he might become the master where he had once been the apprentice—provided his race did not disqualify him.

As for Robert Bridges, had he spotted in James Forten a worthy successor? His treatment of him strongly suggests he had. Barely one year into his apprenticeship, James Forten was promoted to foreman. Robert Bridges's message to his other employees, all of them white, was that they could accept the situation or leave.

Long before he began his apprenticeship, James Forten had learned the basics of sailmaking from his father. Now, with Bridges guiding him, he learned the full range of the sailmaker's craft. To begin with, he needed to know how to judge the quality of the canvas and the cordage he would be working with. Suppliers might try to unload inferior materials on him, and that could lead to a poorly made sail, a canceled order, or even the loss of a vessel at sea. Canvas came in various grades, the lower the number the heavier the canvas. Canvas duck (from the Dutch *doek*) was made of flax, and the best came from the Baltic. That was a problem, and Forten would have heard Bridges complain about the fact that the United States could not produce its own high-grade duck. The lack of a domestic source of supply put the nation at a distinct disadvantage. If a major sea power like Britain or France decided to mount a blockade, the United States would be starved of its vital supplies of Baltic canvas. A solution to the problem was at least three decades away when James Forten began his apprenticeship.

There were other supplies that needed to be bought for the loft. The bolt-rope—of the best Baltic hemp—that was sewn around the head, foot, and leeches (sides) of a sail had to be strong enough to take the strain, but not spun so tightly that it was difficult to sew. The sewing twine had to be of the finest quality. The beeswax and turpentine that went into the concoction James had boiled up in the sail-loft for waxing the twine when he had come to work with his father had to be the genuine articles. Smell and feel would help James Forten, the apprentice sailmaker, judge their quality.

As a day-laborer in the sail-loft, Forten had sewn together "cloths" or panels of canvas as they were handed to him. He had watched sails being designed, but he had played no role in that process. Once he embarked on his apprenticeship, an important part of his education was learning how to measure sails. For a vessel that Bridges worked on regularly, that was simple. He kept a record of the measurements of each sail. He could fill an order for a new fore-topsail or mizzen-topgallant while the ship was still at sea and have it ready when she came into port.

When it came to fitting out a new vessel, precise measurements were needed. A sailor could be assigned to climb the rigging and call down the measurements, but it made more sense for the sailmaker or his assistant to do it. Robert Bridges had never been a sailor. James Forten had. He had been aloft on the *Royal Louis* with a British warship in hot pursuit. He had helped trim the sails of the *Commerce* as she pitched and rolled in the North Atlantic. Climbing the rigging of a vessel, yardstick, pencil, and notebook at the ready, as she lay at anchor in the Delaware was child's play.

Once the sailmaker had his measurements, he could begin designing the sail. Forten learned the use of drafting tools—the small ones for the paper plan and the much larger ones used on the loft floor. Scale drawings were made first. Then the design was transferred full-scale to the floor of the loft and drawn out in chalk. Eventually the bolts of canvas would be unrolled, cut with a knife, and marked to indicate where each panel belonged in the composition of the sail.

In designing any sail, and especially in looking over the sail-plan for a new vessel, a sailmaker had to ask lots of questions. What use would a particular sail be put to? How long might the vessel remain at sea? What weather conditions might she encounter? A sail that was to withstand a typhoon in the South China Sea might need to be made differently from a sail that was expected to cope with a freezing gale in the North Atlantic. Again, practical knowledge of how a sail handled under different conditions was crucial.

With plenty of orders on hand—and Robert Bridges was among the most successful sailmakers in the city—the loft was a hive of activity. Suppliers and ships' captains were in and out all day long. As for the work force, several dozen men and boys were employed at any one time. Every workplace had its own peculiar sounds, and the sounds of the sail-loft were distinctive. Accompanying the buzz of conversation was the click of metal on metal as the men used the "eyes" on their palms to push their needles through the canvas.

Typical Sail Loft Floor With Pieces of Sail
James Forten would have been very familiar with a scene like this—
with various parts of a sail waiting to be stitched together.

When the sail had been assembled, the work of making it function properly began. Different parts of a sail needed additional strengthening. Then there was the rope-work to be done. The first stage was the adding to square sails of reef-points and reef-bands.

These rows of strings or laces would be used to reduce or increase the spread of a sail. In a gale no captain wanted his sails fully extended. They would make the vessel unwieldy and could even cause her to capsize. His crew would have to go aloft to tie all or part of each sail to the yard using the reef-points. When the storm subsided, the command would be given to "out reefs," and the weary crew would go aloft again to unfasten the reef-points. James Forten knew from personal experience exactly how reefs were used.

It was the bolt-rope sewn around the edges of a sail that transformed it from a two-dimensional to a three-dimensional object. Roping was a highly skilled job. One had to know what weight of rope to use, what thickness of twine to sew it on with, and how much of a twist to put in it. There were printed tables one could use, but the master sailmaker knew by instinct and experience what was wanted.

There was more to be done than measuring the bolt-rope and sewing it on. Various fittings needed to be made to protect it from the elements and reduce wear and tear. There were loops to be worked in the rope for fastening the end of a line and hauling the sail up to the yard. There were grommets to be inserted for lines and fittings. The task of completing a full suit of sails could keep a team of sailmakers employed for weeks. Thousands of square feet of canvas and hundreds of yards of rope would be used. The true test of the quality of a particular loft's work would come when a vessel returned from Europe or Asia with her sails intact and wearing well.

In the thirteen years he trained him, Robert Bridges taught James Forten to work with a wide variety of rigs—schooners for the West Indian trade, brigs for coasting, ocean-going square-riggers for the trade with Europe and Asia. Like other sailmakers, he would be expected to know how to manufacture wind-sails. At sea in hot climates these large canvas tubes would be lowered into the hold to provide air for both men and cargo. Sailmakers also made awnings to shield crew and cargo from the elements. Bridges taught Forten how to fashion canvas "coats" to protect the masts and rudder, and a host of other items not intended for shipboard use. Sailmakers made tents and hoses. They made speaking-trumpets. They made covers, bags, and tarpaulins of all sorts and all sizes. In short, if something could be made from canvas, a sailmaker would try to make it.

The partnership between Robert Bridges and James Forten was a mutually productive one. Bridges taught Forten all he knew and introduced him to the merchants and ship-owners who gave the firm its commissions. In return, Forten contributed an important perspective. He had been to sea in peace and war. He had learned a great deal about handling canvas under sail. He had also seen much larger vessels than Bridges had ever set eyes on. As she sailed up the Thames, the *Commerce* had been dwarfed by 700-ton monsters employed in the East India trade. Ships of that size were simply not seen in American ports in the 1780s and 1790s. Above all, James Forten understood the rigors of a sailor's life. He knew about canvas as someone who worked with it on the loft floor and in the rigging of a trans-Atlantic trader.

One of the stories handed down about James Forten is that he patented a device for handling sails. He may well have studied a certain problem and invented a new technique or piece of machinery, but he never secured a patent. No patent was registered to him, or to Bridges as his employer. But then there were plenty of inventions that were never actually patented.

And if James Forten *had* invented something that gave the Bridges loft a competitive edge, it would certainly explain a remarkably generous act on Robert Bridges's part. In 1792 he bought a house for Forten. He handed over £250 Pennsylvania money for a two-story house on Shippen Street in Southwark, the district just outside the city where most of the shipyards and related workshops were located. The arrangement was that Bridges would hold the actual deed until Forten was able to pay him back. The house was small and probably rather crowded. It sheltered Forten, his mother, his sister, her husband, and the growing brood of young Dunbars. Still, when many working men and women, black and white, remained renters all their lives, James Forten was a homeowner, and Robert Bridges had helped him achieve that status.

"A View of the New Market from the Corner of Shippen & Second Streets, Philadelphia, 1787"
Engraving by James Thackara. Published (1830) by Robert Desilver.
(Library Company of Philadelphia)
This was what the Shippen Street neighborhood looked like around the time that Robert Bridges helped James Forten buy a home there.

In 1798 Robert Bridges retired. For James Forten everything had been leading up to this—the training he had received, the growing dependence on him by Bridges in the day-to-day running of the loft, the introductions to old established customers. When the employees in the loft realized Forten was about to take over the business, they split into two camps. All the apprentices announced that they would be staying. Their indentures had been drawn up with Robert Bridges, but increasingly James Forten had been responsible for their training. They were content with that arrangement. In essence, they were saying that they judged him skilled enough to continue teaching them. The journeymen were not so sure about staying. They had finished their apprenticeships, and they were free to come and go as they wished. They were worried not so much about Forten's level of expertise as they were about his ability to retain Bridges's customers, keep the sail-loft a going concern, and pay them on a regular basis. There was no other economic enterprise of this size and complexity being run by a black man in all of Philadelphia. Robert Bridges came to the rescue. Maybe he won over the journeymen with assurances of full order-books. Maybe he arranged a loan for Forten. We don't know exactly what he did. A friend of James Forten's observed simply that Bridges helped him and the journeymen stayed.

Another crucial factor was the patronage of the firm of Willing & Francis. The Bridges loft was on the upper floor of one of the partners' warehouses. Because they had already employed Bridges and knew the quality of the work his loft produced, the partners gave Forten some of his first orders. They were rich and powerful merchants, and they owned or part-owned numerous vessels. Their confidence in James Forten earned him more customers.

Robert Bridges died on January 18, 1800. James Forten attended his funeral at Christ Church and probably closed the sail-loft for a few hours as a mark of respect. Bridges had treated him as a trusted junior partner and a friend. James Forten never forgot that, but now he was on his own, to make his way as best he could among Philadelphia's master-craftsmen and merchants. Would they regard him as Robert Bridges had done, as a skilled craftsman and a knowledgeable man of business who happened to be black? Or would they see him first and foremost as a man of color? Time alone would tell.

CHAPTER SEVEN

South Wharves

By the mid-1830s James Forten's sail-loft at 95 South Wharves was a show-place of his industry and his values. All sorts of people came to call, intrigued by reports of his wealth and by the all-too-rare sight of a racially integrated workforce presided over by a man of color. Black and white men worked harmoniously together in what James Forten insisted was a model for American society as a whole. His order-books were full, and he was one of the city's leading sailmakers. He also had interests beyond the sail-loft. Real estate, loans at interest, and stock in banks, railroads, and canals steadily increased his fortune. However, as he was quick to point out to his visitors, he had struggled in those early years after he took over the sail-loft. He had faced tough times, but his friends had stood by him, and he never forgot a favor.

To have a sense of how James Forten rose to prominence as a businessman, we need to ask a whole series of questions. To begin with, how significant a factor was his race? Who employed him? Whom did he employ? How did he treat his workers? What was life like in and around the sail-loft? And how, why, and when did James Forten branch out to become not just a successful sailmaker but an astute man of business with wide-ranging interests?

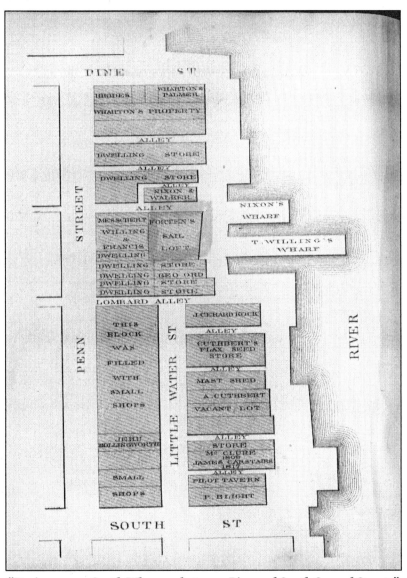

"Businesses on South Wharves, between Pine and South Second Streets"
From Abraham Ritter, *Philadelphia and Her Merchants* (1860).
Library Company of Philadelphia.
This map by a white merchant who knew James Forten
shows where his sail-loft was located.

There were some things about James Forten's long career in business that had nothing whatsoever to do with the fact that he was a man of color. Like other members of Philadelphia's business community, his fortunes rose and fell with the economy of the city, the region, and the nation. When trade was flourishing, he and his fellow merchants made money. When the economy went into a tail-spin, as it did again and again over the years, everyone suffered. And then there were the local factors. After 1800 Philadelphia was no longer the nation's capital, nor was it the capital of Pennsylvania, and that had an impact. Even the climate and the location were issues. Although a seaport, Philadelphia is a hundred miles from the open ocean. The Delaware could and did freeze in wintertime, and trade literally came to a standstill. Of course, that could be an excellent time to refurbish a vessel's sails, so the sail-loft could literally weather a deep freeze—as long as it did not last too long. With the ups and downs in the market, the uncertainty of the weather, and all sorts of issues beyond his control, James Forten knew it paid to be cautious. On the other hand, he realized there were times when a shrewd investor could make good money—and he was as shrewd as anyone in business along the Philadelphia waterfront.

James Forten's earliest patrons were the partners in the firm of Willing & Francis. He acknowledged their help and trust by naming one of his sons in their honor. But who were his other customers? One can guess who some of his friends in the mercantile community were. There was William Deas, after whom Forten named another son. There were also the members of the Bridges family. Robert Bridges's son, Culpepper, did as his father had hoped and became a merchant. He was the part-owner of a couple of vessels. Three of Robert Bridges's daughters married men who were merchants and ship-owners. Given that Culpepper Bridges had known James Forten most of his life and had had ample opportunity to see the quality of his work, it would have been surprising if Forten had *not* received commissions from him. And Culpepper was in a position to recommend him to his brothers-in-law.

Another friend was Irishman Patrick Hayes. He had extensive interests in the China trade and in commerce with Cuba. He and Forten had a good working relationship. Hayes paid his bills on time and knew first-class work when he saw it. There were also small gestures of friendship between the two men. On one occasion Hayes brought back a box of cigars for Forten from Cuba. On another occasion Forten had his men make a canvas cover for the captain's piano.

James Forten counted other businessmen and ship-owners among his friends. Again and again in his letters he referred to individuals, like iron merchant Thomas Ash, or to unnamed men among the seafaring fraternity who supplied him with news of happenings in distant ports. From his acquaintances Forten amassed a wealth of information about the world of business in general, and that enabled him to make sound decisions about the running of the sail-loft and about his various investments.

Many shippers and merchants liked James Forten and, to a limited extent, socialized with him. Well-to-do Philadelphia Quaker Susanna Emlen described to a relative in England how some of the leading businessmen in the city had called to congratulate Forten on his marriage and drink a celebratory glass of punch with him. Abraham Ritter, who wrote a fascinating book about the business community of early 19th century Philadelphia, the era when he himself was starting out, recalled James Forten as "a gentleman by nature, easy in manner...affable...[and] popular." He had been "well received by the gentlemen of lighter shade." Beyond Emlen's passing reference and Ritter's thumbnail sketch there are stray references to white businessmen greeting Forten in the street. "Though he belonged to a proscribed race," wrote one of his contemporaries, "it was no uncommon thing to see him shaking hands, or walking arm in arm, with merchants of the first respectability."

There is much more, though, that one would like to know. How did his business relationships begin and progress? Who called upon him at his place of business, and who visited him in the more intimate setting of his home? Who took him by the hand and who greeted him in the street? And who refused outright to do business with him because he was black? That there were some merchants who gossiped about him behind his back and insinuated that he was getting above himself we know—Abraham Ritter, whose map appears at the beginning of the chapter, said as much, and so did others—but did such attitudes stem from racism, from jealousy, or from a mix of the two? And did those attitudes impact on James Forten's ability to make money? These are questions we need to ponder, but they are questions we cannot really answer because people seldom leave written records of their innermost thoughts and feelings—and sometimes they are not even aware of what makes them think and act as they do.

We are on firmer ground when we look at James Forten and his workers. We know because he stated it outright that he was determined from the moment he took control of the sail-loft that his workforce would be an interracial one. He kept Bridges's workers, all of whom were white. He also took on white youths who came to him in search of apprenticeships. He set certain ground-rules, though. He paid his workers and he expected them to defer to him in certain matters. That deference went far beyond arriving for work on time and laboring faithfully at their assigned tasks. For instance, James Forten considered himself perfectly justified in telling his white employees how to vote and making sure they did as he told them.

We do not know the names of any of his white workers, although we do know by Forten's own account that several of them worked for him life-long. For a variety of reasons, his African American workers are easier to identify. Some were family members. Others were friends or the sons or brothers of friends. For instance, Forten's ties with black New England shipper Paul Cuffe brought him two apprentices. When Cuffe's widowed daughter, Ruth Howard, married New Bedford merchant Richard Johnson, a widower originally from Philadelphia, both had children from their previous marriages. When it came time to find good trades for their sons, Ruth and Richard contacted a man they both knew well. Ezra Rothschild Johnson and his stepbrother, Shadrach Howard, were packed off to Philadelphia to board with the Forten family and learn the sailmaker's craft in James Forten's loft.

Black or white, to work for James Forten meant to accept his authority. We know from tax records that he owned an expensive gold watch, and he used it to enforce punctuality. He did not permit the use of alcohol in his workplace. A workman who spent his lunch-break in a tavern or kept a bottle in his lunch-pail was unlikely to do careful work. However, for James Forten it was more than a question of preventing costly mistakes. He believed drinking was a sign of moral weakness and he would not tolerate it, any more than he would swearing, Sabbath-breaking, gambling, or a host of other forms of what he saw as "vice."

Life in the sail-loft was seldom dull, though. News flew back and forth along the wharves about ship arrivals and departures, which vessel was carrying what cargo, and what the latest reports were about conditions in foreign and domestic markets. James Forten's workplace, like every other workplace along the Delaware, was a hub of gossip and business intelligence. He and his workers also witnessed the hazards of life on the waterfront. Men tumbled from the rigging of ships, lost limbs in horrific accidents, and were killed as derricks collapsed or heavy loads fell and crushed them. Drownings were frequent because few people could swim. James

Forten *could* swim, and on a number of occasions he plucked people out of the water. Several of his rescues took place during the winter months, when he risked hypothermia as well as drowning. In 1821 the Humane Society of Philadelphia presented him with a certificate in recognition of his heroism. He had it framed and hung in his sitting-room. When an English visitor dined with the Fortens some years later, he inquired about the certificate. James Forten told him he was very proud of it and would not part with it for a thousand dollars.

Certificate from the Humane Society of Pennsylvania
Certificate Flatfile, Historical Society of Pennsylvania.
The certificate awarded him for his river rescues
was one of James Forten's prize possessions.

By the early 1820s James Forten's pursuit of wealth clashed with his antislavery beliefs in an unlikely fashion. He had learned his craft working with flaxen sail-duck imported from the Baltic and the Netherlands. However, there were obvious dangers for a country that was so dependent on an imported commodity. Americans learned that the hard way during the Napoleonic Wars and the War of 1812, when British blockades in Europe and then along America's own shores meant supplies of canvas could not get through and vessels were trapped in port because they lacked sails.

For various reasons, although the United States could not produce flaxen canvas in sufficient quantity and at an attractive price, it could produce cotton canvas. People began experimenting and found that cotton sails were just as good as flaxen sails, but for James Forten and others who felt as he did about the existence of slavery, that posed a moral and ethical dilemma. Cotton was cultivated by slaves. If they used slave-produced goods, weren't they in essence putting money in the pockets of Southern planters? James Forten was trapped. If he refused to use cotton he would have to stop making sails, and that meant he would be out of business. What should he do? In the end, he went over to using cotton, reflecting perhaps that slavery was kept alive by something far more basic than dollars and cents. It thrived on the fundamental belief in the superiority of some people and the inferiority of others. The best he could do was to dedicate a good part of his profits to changing hearts and minds and hastening the coming of the day when the nation as a whole would reject slavery as immoral and a violation of human rights. He loathed slavery, but he knew a bankrupt abolitionist could do nothing to bring about its end. Even so, he was compromising with the slave power of the South and its Northern supporters, and he knew it.

CHAPTER EIGHT

A Talent for Making Money

Although the sail-loft was at the center of James Forten's business empire, his interests extended far beyond it. Like any shrewd businessman, he did not want his money lying idle. Always looking for a good investment, he had begun by the early 1800s to divert some of his capital into making loans at interest. Standard practice today for someone in search of a short-term loan for a commercial venture is to go to a bank. People did the same thing in Forten's time, but the banking industry in America was in its infancy, and anyway banks had a nasty habit of going broke. So what did people do? They looked for other people with money to lend, and they talked. "Business" had an uncanny way of minimizing the importance of race. For someone like James Forten, who wanted to make his money work for him, a loan of a couple of hundred dollars at the standard six percent a year interest was a good investment. Naturally, he had to be certain the individual borrowing from him could pay back the loan (with interest) when it came due. Over the years, though, he made many loans—to neighbors, to friends, to friends of friends, and sometimes to virtual strangers—and usually they paid him back. When they did not, he knew what he must do.

Hardly a greedy man, Forten would generally give borrowers more time to settle up, but he had to draw a line somewhere. If necessary, he was ready to go to court. His lawyers were white men for the simple reason that there were no African American members of the Bar. The men he hired were men he trusted—Richard Rush, and when he gave up his practice to go into politics, Richard Peters Sr. and his nephew, Richard Jr., and finally a Quaker, Thomas Earle. Although all were antislavery to some degree, their commitment varied. Whether fiery abolitionists or simply men who thought the nation would be better off without slavery, they were happy to work with James Forten, and he was equally happy to have them on his side. Hardly a year went by when he did not have some legal matter to deal with—a case in one or other of the Philadelphia courts, a deed to be drawn up, or a polite but to-the-point letter to be sent to an individual or a business that had ignored his request to repay a loan.

For over two decades James Forten was a well-known presence in the Philadelphia District Court and the Court of Common Pleas. His lawyers handled the various lawsuits, but he liked to be on hand to keep an eye on things. No one ever suggested that he should not have been there or that he had no right to sue white debtors. After all, if *his* rights were not secure, then no one else's were, and the whole debtor-creditor network was threatened. James Forten was cynical enough, or perhaps just realistic enough, to appreciate that money spoke a language that was universal.

In addition to money-lending, he speculated in real estate. Within five years of taking over the sail-loft, he had saved enough to begin investing. He already owned the house on Shippen Street that Robert Bridges had bought for him. In 1803 Forten purchased a piece of land on nearby George Street. Then he hired a house-carpenter. The two men settled on a price and a time-table, and Forten left the house-carpenter to complete the job. When the house was finished, Forten found a decent tenant for it and started collecting the rent.

In 1806 came the purchase of a fine three-story brick house on Third and Lombard Streets. James Forten moved his family into the home, and it remained in their possession for the next eighty years. He did not sell the Shippen Street house. Instead he leased it out, and it became another of his rental properties.

Over the next few years James Forten acquired more investment property. In 1809 he bought another house on Lombard Street and rented it out. On the eve of the War of 1812 he made one substantial investment and a much smaller one. The smaller one was in Blockley Township, an area just outside the city that he knew was ripe for development. The larger investment must have taken a sizable chunk of his capital. He paid over six thousand dollars for a house and lot on South Ninth Street. It was a calculated gamble, but the house proved one of the most profitable of Forten's rental properties. He followed up with more purchases—a house and land on Lombard Street in 1813, and another nearby piece of property later that same year.

In the years that followed, he snapped up more real estate. He had a good head for business. He knew when someone was in trouble. He went to sheriff's sales and picked up a house here or a parcel of land there. He juggled various properties, selling when he could get a good price or he had another project for which he needed capital. He might sell outright, or he might give a buyer a mortgage if that person seemed trustworthy. Honest and straightforward he might be, but he was in business to make money.

James Forten was a substantial landlord, and his tenants represented a cross-section of Philadelphia society—a teacher, a couple of ships' captains, an accountant, a self-described "gentleman," a carter, a soap manufacturer, a man who ran an employment office, a ladies' hat-maker, and many more. His main concern was not race or gender, but paying the rent on time.

His growing wealth and prestige within the business community gave James Forten power, and he used it. Others made use of it as well. For example, when he was in trouble, African American sailor William Wright turned to Forten as someone he believed had both the inclination and the ability to help him. In July 1822 Wright sailed out of Philadelphia on the brig *George,* captained by James Gaul. They were on their way back from the West Indies in October when the vessel put in at New Castle, in the slave state of Delaware, and Gaul placed Wright in the local jail, "he says for Safe keeping." Wright feared that Gaul meant to sell him as a slave. As soon as he could secure a pen and some paper, he wrote a brief note explaining his plight to "Mr. James Fortune, Sailmaker," of Philadelphia, and got a friend to take it upriver for him. How did Wright and Forten know one another? James Forten counted many seafaring men among his circle of friends, and he often employed sailors in his loft to do basic sewing. In his estimation of Forten's readiness to help him, Wright was correct. Forten passed the note to one of the officers of the Pennsylvania Abolition Society, and Wright was restored to his family.

James Forten's status and business knowledge helped others in less dramatic fashion. He assisted friends in the African American community when they made their wills. He acted as their executor, and in one or two cases he agreed to become the guardian of their children. Some of those friends were sailors setting out on voyages from which they feared they might never return. Others belonged to Forten's church, and still others were simply acquaintances from the growing free black community. All of them knew that James Forten could be trusted. African American organizations elected him to their boards. He served on the vestry of his church, and his duties included negotiating loans for the church and advising on investments. He was an officer of the African Masonic Lodge, and its records are full of references to his handling of finances. He helped coordinate the raising of funds to support black schools and colleges. He gave white abolitionists tips on the marketing of antislavery publications. In short, what James Forten did not know about making, handling, and investing money was probably not worth knowing, and he put that knowledge to the service of his growing family, his community, and the causes that meant so much to him.

CHAPTER NINE

Raising a Family in Freedom

In an era when most free men, black or white, married for the first time in their early- to mid-twenties, James Forten was unusual. He was still a bachelor when he was in his late thirties. Remaining single wasn't really a matter of choice. Becoming a master craftsman and establishing himself in business left little money or time to spare for a wife and children. And then there were his existing obligations. Margaret Forten had labored long and hard to support herself and her children. But for her, the family would have been destitute. Her son would certainly not have had any formal education and would probably have spent his entire life among the ranks of the laboring poor. As James Forten prospered, he was concerned to make sure his mother enjoyed the security she had struggled to provide for him and his sister.

Then there was Abigail and her family. James knew how low a sailor's pay was. William Dunbar was away for months at a time. Even if he could get an advance on his wages, Abigail and the children would barely be able to make ends meet while he was at sea. James did what he could for Abigail and William, offering them a home until the Dunbar family outgrew the small house on Shippen

Street. When they moved into lodgings, he helped them financially. In 1799 Abigail gave birth to her fourth child. She and William named him James Forten Dunbar in acknowledgement of past favors and in the hope that his uncle might take a special interest in him.

Eventually James Forten felt secure enough to begin looking around for a wife. Martha Beatte, seventeen years his junior, was from Darby Township, several miles downriver from Philadelphia. How the couple met we do not know. Possibly Martha (known to friends and family as Patty) came to the city in search of work, or perhaps business took James to Darby. However they met, they courted, and on the evening of November 10, 1803, at St. Thomas's African Episcopal Church, Absalom Jones united them in marriage. In less than a year from that joyous occasion, Rev. Jones was called upon to conduct Patty Forten's funeral.

Soon after Patty's death another tragedy befell the Forten family. William Dunbar died. James set aside his plans to marry again. He had to do what he could for Abigail and her family. They would have a home with him as long as they needed one. The Dunbars lived with him for years, and when the last of her children ventured out on his own, James moved Abigail into one of his smaller properties and told her she could live there rent-free for the rest of her life.

James Forten married off his niece, Margaret, to one of his apprentices, George Lewis, a young free black man from Delaware. He also found room in the sail-loft for his nephews. Nicholas proved a disappointment. He eventually went to sea, jumped ship in the West Indies, and was never heard of again. William Jr. was very different from his brother. He trained as a sailmaker with his uncle and then went to sea. The fact that he knew how to repair sails meant he earned higher pay than many of the other men he sailed with. Captains were glad to have a crew member with

William's skills. The youngest of the Dunbars, James, was only six when his father died. He stayed with Abigail for a few years and began helping out around the sail-loft, but at age eleven he went to sea. In the years that followed, he traveled the world, from the West Indies to Europe and to Asia, and when he was back in Philadelphia for any length of time he knew he always had a job waiting for him in the sail-loft.

Charlotte Vandine Forten
Francis J. Grimké Papers, Moorland-Spingarn Research Center,
Howard University
This photograph of James Forten's second wife was taken when she was
very old. She lived for almost one hundred years.

His brother-in-law's death and the plight of his sister and her children obliged James Forten to remain single for a while longer, but on December 10, 1805 he married for a second time. Charlotte Vandine was of African, Native American and European ancestry, and at 20 she was half James's age. James moved his new bride into the house on Shippen Street that he shared with his mother. Sadly, Margaret Forten died the following spring. At age 84 her death was not unexpected. Still, her presence as the matriarch of the family was sadly missed.

Less than six months after his mother's death, James Forten completed the purchase of his new home, 92 Lombard Street. It was in the Lombard Street home on September 11, 1806 that James and Charlotte's first child was born. A girl, she was christened Margaretta, or "little Margaret," in memory of her grandmother. In November 1808 Charlotte gave birth to a second daughter. Named for her mother, little Charlotte died on March 24, 1814 of hydrocephalus. On February 1, 1810 a third daughter was born. She was baptized Harriet Davy Forten, a tribute to someone who had meant a lot to James Forten. Back when he had been Robert Bridges's foreman, he had befriended Harriet Bridges. She was a toddler when he first met her. She had grown up, married merchant Robert Broome Davy, and died young. James Forten had been fond of her and now he showed his affection by naming his daughter after her. On November 15, 1811 Charlotte presented James with a long-awaited son, James, Jr. Another son, born on May 12, 1813, was baptized Robert Bridges Forten in memory of James Forten's benefactor. A fourth daughter, Sarah Louisa, was born in 1814, and a fifth, Mary Isabella, just a year later. Then along came another son. He was named Thomas in honor of James's father and given the middle names Willing Francis as a sign of respect for the partners in the firm of Willing & Francis who had helped James Forten in his early years in business. The Fortens' ninth and last child, another son, was born in 1823 when Charlotte was 39 and James 57. In selecting a name, James paid tribute to another white man, by then long dead. William Deas had trusted him to make sails for his vessels, and James Forten never forgot that vote of confidence. Naming his son William Deas Forten was his way of saying thank you.

The Forten home was crowded, but far less so than the miserable hovels in the poorer quarters of the city. In 1810 James Forten presided over a household of fifteen. A decade later there were eighteen people in the home, and by 1830 that total had risen to 22. Not all of them were "family" in the strict sense of the word, but they were "family" as James Forten understood the term. Who were these unrelated men and women who lived under his roof? We know about a couple of them. In 1805, Forten took on a 15-year-old African American apprentice from Maryland, Samuel Elbert. Samuel lived with Forten and his mother on Shippen Street and

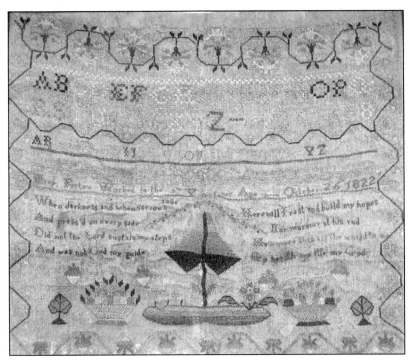

Sampler Stitched by Mary Isabella Forten
From Huey Family Collection
Mary was just six years old in 1822 when she sewed her sampler.

then moved with the family to 92 Lombard. Six years later the Fortens got a servant to help Charlotte with her household duties. Judy—no last name appeared in the record—lived with them for eleven years. Over time Samuel and Judy would have their successors—servants, apprentices, and journeymen, all of whom formed part of James Forten's extended family.

From the first, Charlotte and James Forten were determined to give their children a good education, but the issue they had to confront was the same one faced by other well-to-do black parents. How could they get their children an education that would prepare them to be more than domestics or unskilled laborers. There were no public schools for black children in Philadelphia until 1822. Private academies would not admit them, while the charity schools for black children offered only the basics. James and Charlotte refused to give up. They joined forces with another African American couple, Grace and Robert Douglass. The Fortens and the Douglasses pooled their resources, hired a teacher, and began their own school. It was a success, and other affluent black parents enrolled their children.

With the exception of Mary Isabella, who was an invalid most of her life, the Forten daughters attended this school until they were in their mid-teens, at which point their father hired tutors to teach them music and French at home. They also read extensively. Like their sisters, the Forten boys were educated at the school their parents and the Douglasses had set up before transferring to the Pennsylvania Abolition Society's new Clarkson School for their high school education.

In addition to their immediate family and their servants and apprentices, the Fortens provided houseroom for wards of one sort or another. On one occasion James brought home to a surprised Charlotte an African prince who had been entrusted to him. The eight-year-old prince stayed only a few days, but another child lived with the Fortens for several years. Ann, the orphaned daughter of James's old friend Jean-Baptiste Appo, remained with the Fortens until her untimely death from tuberculosis. And then there were the Purvises.

Sampler Stitched by Margaretta Forten
From the Huey Family Collection
Margaretta was eleven in 1817 when she stitched this sampler.

The links between the Fortens and Robert and Joseph Purvis were ties of affection rather than legal ties. James and Charlotte had probably met Englishman William Purvis on one of his visits to Philadelphia. Purvis came from the village of Ross, in Northumberland, close to the Scottish border. As a younger son, he stood to inherit very little from his father, so he had come to

America to seek his fortune. He had ended up in South Carolina, in business with another brother, Burridge. Burridge managed their affairs upcountry in Columbia, while William took care of things in Charleston. Although they dealt in many commodities, by far the most profitable was cotton.

In Charleston William shared his home with Harriet Judah, a free woman of color. Purvis family lore had it that Harriet was the daughter of a Moroccan-born slave, Dido Badaracka, and a German Jewish flour merchant, Baron Judah. William and Harriet lived together in Charleston for many years, and it was there that their children were born—William Jr. in 1808, Robert in 1810, and Joseph in 1812. In 1819 William began making plans to retire and buy an estate back in Britain. Married or not, Harriet was his lifelong partner, but there would be difficulties as long as they remained in a place where her ancestry was known. And then there were their sons. He could leave them his fortune, but William knew he could not educate them as gentlemen in South Carolina.

William sent Harriet and the boys to Philadelphia while he started wrapping up his business in South Carolina. By 1821 William Jr., Robert and Joseph were attending the Clarkson School, and it was through the school that they and their mother came to know the Forten boys. The families also met each Sunday at church.

Although his business activities forced William Purvis to spend a great deal of time away from his family, he visited whenever he could. In the fall of 1826 he was staying with Harriet and the children in Philadelphia when he contracted typhus and died. He had made a will, and under its provisions Harriet and the boys became very rich indeed. Harriet got ten thousand dollars worth of stock in the Bank of the United States, while her sons shared an estate valued at a quarter of a million dollars.

Harriet mourned for William for over a year before marrying William Miller, a prominent black minister based in New York City.

Robert and Joseph saw little of their stepfather. They were packed off to Amherst Academy, a preparatory school in Massachusetts linked to nearby Amherst College. Sadly, their brother was too sick to join them. William Jr. was suffering from tuberculosis. By the spring of 1828, when he knew he was dying, he wrote a will leaving all his money and everything he owned to his mother in trust for Robert and Joseph.

In the space of two years Robert and Joseph had lost their father and elder brother. Their mother spent her time in New York with her husband. Was it so surprising that the two young men should have welcomed the chance to become "adopted" members of the Forten family? James and Charlotte were happy to treat them like sons. And if either of these rich and well-educated brothers should happen to take more than a friendly interest in one of their daughters, they would be delighted to have him as a son-in-law.

James Forten could buy his children a first-rate education. He could house his widowed sister comfortably and provide for his mother in her old age. He could give the men of color who worked for him the chance to master a trade and move out of the ranks of the unskilled. He could take in his friends' orphaned children and give his servants a stable life, even if it was one lived under his watchful eye. What he could not do for any of these individuals was to insulate them from the consequences of being black in America. Admittedly some were so light-skinned that whites did not always detect their African ancestry; but when they did, it exposed that individual to everything from muttered insults to violence or enslavement. No member of his household, from the lowliest of his servants to Forten himself, was spared, and he knew it.

James Forten was never enslaved and he knew his children were unlikely to suffer that fate, but slavery did reach out to threaten members of his extended family. Amos Dunbar, the son of his wayward nephew Nicholas, was apprenticed to a man in Pittsburgh in the mid-1820s to learn a trade. At some point the child's mother and stepfather discovered he had been taken to Louisiana and sold as a slave. Great-uncle James came to the rescue. Amos had plucked up the courage to tell Robert Layton, the man who had unwittingly bought him in the slave market in New Orleans, that he was free-born and had a rich relative. Layton was in the shipping business and had heard of the black sailmaker who had made such a name for himself in Philadelphia. If Amos really was related to James Forten, Layton did not want to keep him. A freeborn slave could stir up trouble among Layton's other slaves; and, if that same individual had a rich relative, that relative might be persuaded to part with some cash to get him back. Layton wrote Forten saying he would be happy to free Amos and hinting that some token of appreciation was due.

By the fall of 1825 Amos had regained his freedom. Had he not had a family member with money and influence, he would have lived out his life as a slave. And his case was not the only one in which slavery threatened the Forten family. A relative of Charlotte's almost ended his days on a plantation in Mississippi. He was rescued, but it was a lesson, if James Forten needed one, that every woman and man of color was vulnerable as long as slavery existed anywhere in the nation.

His family was a tremendous source of strength in James Forten's life. Happy in his marriage, proud of his children, he enjoyed his role as husband and father. A man of means, an astute businessman, he could have made his home and his sail-loft the twin centers of his life. And in a sense he did. It was from his family that he drew emotional support and from his place of business that he derived both his sense of pride as a master craftsman and the power that came with the possession of wealth. But James Forten reached beyond his home and his workplace. By the 1820s he was one of the most influential men of color in the United States.

Understanding how he achieved that status, what battles he fought, and what allies and enemies he made along the way is as vital to a sense of who James Forten was as his flair for business and his love for his family.

CHAPTER TEN

A Community Takes Shape

In 1785, when he began his apprenticeship with Robert Bridges, James Forten was one of about fifteen hundred black residents of Philadelphia and its adjoining districts. Whites might see them all as "Africans," but in reality black Philadelphians were a diverse group. Some were foreign-born—people from various parts of Africa and the Caribbean. Then there were the American-born—migrants from every state in the Union, most of them drawn to Philadelphia in the hope of finding work. Sailors and cooks, carters and sweeps, washerwomen and waiters—black men and women seized all those jobs and more, eager for financial independence.

The vast majority of those who made up Philadelphia's rapidly growing free black population had been slaves. While the Gradual Abolition Act had been hailed by many as the beginning of the end for slavery in Pennsylvania, it *was* just a beginning. Only the children of enslaved women benefitted—and only at age 28, after a lengthy period of "apprenticeship" laboring without pay for their mothers' owners, or whomever those owners sold, leased, or bequeathed them to. Of course, for a while James Forten was an apprentice, but not in the same sense that *they* were apprenticed. He had very different expectations. He would become a master of his trade. They would be turned out into the world to fend for themselves, in most cases with no marketable skills and few resources.

Despite the less than complete freedom many black people enjoyed in Philadelphia, the image of the city as a haven of liberty persisted. To the annoyance of many whites, the "African" population increased dramatically in the last years of the eighteenth century, and much of that increase was due to migration. From 2,150 in 1790, the total number of black residents rose to over six thousand by 1800. That figure leaped to well over ten thousand by 1810, with angry whites insisting it was even higher if one counted all the runaway slaves who hid from the census-takers.

The City and Port of Philadelphia
William R. Birch, *The City of Philadelphia* (1800),
Library Company of Philadelphia
As this view of the city shows, when James Forten took over the sail-loft,
Philadelphia was growing rapidly and river trade was thriving.

The black migrants who headed to Philadelphia from all points of the compass did so because they believed it offered so much more than they were leaving behind. For many the dream failed to match the reality. However, the picture was not one of unrelieved gloom. Black craftsmen and small-scale shopkeepers made a decent living for themselves and their families. They bought real estate. They sought education for themselves and their children. And they looked with hope to a brighter future. The churches, the schools, the African Lodge, and the benevolent societies they created spoke of optimism, not despair. And in the thick of the development of those institutions was James Forten, a young man who saw his future as very promising indeed.

Interacting with "African" men and women from many different backgrounds was one dimension of James Forten's life. Being caught up in momentous events that impacted all of Philadelphia's residents regardless of race was another. To begin with, he was in Philadelphia in 1787. He saw the likes of George Washington, Benjamin Franklin, James Madison, and Alexander Hamilton, men of note from all thirteen states of the Union, walking or riding to their lodgings, going to dine at this or that tavern, or socializing with old friends during the hours when they were not closeted behind locked doors and shuttered windows in the State House to debate who knew what ...although Forten and his fellow Philadelphians had a pretty shrewd idea that some revision of the Articles of Confederation was being contemplated.

Anyone who expected harmony to prevail with the adoption of the Constitution was sadly mistaken. Over the next decade—and especially after 1790, when the city once more became the nation's capital—mob violence was common in Philadelphia. A highly partisan press indulged in an orgy of character assassination, and Federalists and Republicans denounced one another as traitors to the country's interest.

The first major crisis began with news of a freedom movement an ocean away. In 1789 Philadelphians, together with people across the new nation, were thrilled to learn of the storming of the Bastille. As the uprising in France grew in intensity, sweeping from power America's old ally, Louis XVI, and all that he stood for, the liberty-loving James Forten may have hoped for great things. He understood all too well, though, that revolutions had a way of affecting places and people far from the scene of unrest, and he witnessed the turmoil caused in his native city as the French Revolution proceeded on its bloody course, threatening to involve the United States, since the country was allied with France, and France was soon embroiled in a war with Britain.

The French Revolution was not the only revolution that had repercussions in the United States. Toward the end of 1791, rumors of momentous happenings in the French West Indian colony of Saint Domingue reached Philadelphia. In the following months the rumors were confirmed as a steady trickle of refugees began arriving. The colony's slaves had risen up and were slaughtering their masters. Working in Robert Bridges's sail-loft on the banks of the Delaware, James Forten may have been one of the first Philadelphians to hear of the rebellion. He may even have spoken with sailors who had seen the rebels.

The trickle of refugees from Saint Domingue soon became a flood. Two thousand French men, women, and children crowded into Philadelphia. Thousands more sought safety in other East Coast cities. Quite a few brought slaves with them—those who had been unable to make their escape and join the rebel forces. *Their* arrival was a lesson to white Philadelphians that not all "Africans" were alike. These newcomers looked different. They spoke Creole or Yoruba or Ibo. And not surprisingly they seemed restless, discontented with their lot.

The open warfare between the planters and their slaves on Saint

Domingue not only brought to Philadelphia white slave-owners and some of their bondmen and—women. It also brought people from the colony's small but influential free community of color. James Forten worshipped at the African Church with *gens de couleur* like Jean-Baptiste and Ann Appo and members of the Depee and Duterte families. He heard about their lives on Saint Domingue as people "in between"—neither black nor white, since most were the children of African women and French men. Most of those who were free and affluent owed their freedom and their wealth to their white fathers. Of course, white Philadelphians left the Depees and other *gens de couleur* in no doubt that in Philadelphia they were "Africans."

James Forten never mentioned the yellow fever epidemic of 1793 and his role, if he had one, in relieving the sufferings of its victims, although he was in Philadelphia throughout the crisis. It took time for him and others to realize what was happening. Summer tended to be a sickly season. The humid air seemed to breed illnesses. But this year the mortality rate was far higher. Dozens of graves were being dug each day in every one of the city's churchyards. The numbers were rising alarmingly, and all of the dead seemed to have succumbed to the same dreadful affliction. Finally people awoke to the reality that after a thirty-year absence the yellow fever had returned, brought by the Saint Dominguan refugees.

Dr. Benjamin Rush, the city's leading physician, blamed the outbreak on the noxious "miasma" from a cargo of coffee rotting on one of the wharves. Other observers cited different causes. Some did actually identify the refugees as the source of the contagion, and noted that outbreaks of yellow fever were rare in northern climes, but distressingly common in the West Indies. Debate raged over the best cure—Rush's blood-letting or the use of quinine bark, wine, and cold baths. Arguing over causes and cures did nothing to lessen the toll the disease was taking.

As the grim tally rose, the government all but collapsed as President Washington and most of his cabinet fled the capital, along with anyone else who could afford to do so. On Shippen Street, where James Forten, his mother, and his sister and her family lived, nineteen houses were shut up. The Fortens and the Dunbars stayed. Only when the first frosts came, killing off the mosquitoes that carried the disease from one person to another, did the epidemic loosen its grip, and by then some four thousand people were dead. No one who lived through it ever forgot that dreadful summer, with dead-carts carrying away victims, men and women lying where they had fallen in the streets, the shrieks of the bereaved, and the stench of death and decay that hung over Philadelphia.

Ironically, in the early stages of the outbreak it appeared that there was one segment of the population that was spared. Black residents seemed to be unaffected. To the abolitionist Benjamin Rush this suggested a heaven-sent initiative. He urged white citizens to hire black people to nurse them and their families, and at the same time he told African Americans they had a wonderful opportunity before them. When the epidemic finally ran its course, Philadelphians would be a united people, with grateful whites eager to repay every kindness shown them by their black neighbors. Unfortunately, Rush was mistaken in his belief that black people were immune. They might not have been as susceptible as whites, but a good many caught the fever and died.

If James Forten and his family had responded to Rush's call for help, they had good reason to feel insulted by the aspersions cast upon the black nurses and other relief workers by Mathew Carey. The white publisher alleged that they stole from their patients and demanded unrealistically high payments for any services they rendered. Outraged, Richard Allen and Absalom Jones, two African American men James Forten knew and respected, published a rebuttal. Most of the nurses were poor, they pointed out. People offered them high wages, and they were hardly at fault in accepting what was freely offered, especially given the awful nature of the disease. And if there were a few blacks who neglected or robbed their patients, there were plenty of whites who had done the same. They also pointed out that some black people, regarding it as their Christian duty to reach out to those in need, had refused to take a cent for helping their white neighbors.

The yellow fever returned in 1794 and in 1797. James Forten was among those who believed the only way to prevent yet another recurrence was for Philadelphians to practice "virtue." In the early weeks of 1798, he and Absalom Jones, acting on behalf of the newly established African Church, joined members of fifteen white

Reverend Richard Allen
James Forten worked with the Reverend Richard Allen many times
over the years to address the needs and concerns of the
African American community.

churches in petitioning the state legislature. The city was a pit of sin, they insisted. Drinking, gambling, swearing, disregard for the Sabbath, and even nude bathing in the Delaware were an affront to good order. The only way to ward off another "awful visitation" was to clean up the city in terms of its morality. Alas, nothing the state legislature could do by way of outlawing what the petitioners saw as objectionable behavior was enough to guard against further outbreaks of yellow fever.

James Forten came fairly late to the African Church but, as the "moral order" petition indicates, within a few years he was one of its most influential members. He might have started out as a member of the Free African Society, the mutual benefit organization founded in 1787 by a group of black men led by Absalom Jones and Richard Allen, but at no point was he named one of its officers. If he was a member, he was a very low-ranking one.

Jones and Allen had far-reaching plans for the society. They hoped it would grow into an interdenominational church for Philadelphia's black population. Allen had already made a name for himself as a Methodist preacher when he was invited to come to Philadelphia to preach to the growing body of black Methodists who worshipped at St. George's Methodist Episcopal Church. Impressed by the number of black people in the city, and by the fact that, while hundreds were scattered among the predominantly white congregations, many belonged to no church whatsoever, Allen and Jones hoped one day to create a black church that would come closer to meeting the spiritual needs of "Africans" than they felt any white church could do.

James Forten was not with Jones, Allen, and two of their friends one Sunday in 1792 when they were attending morning service at St. George's. The foursome had been worshipping there for several years, as had scores of other people of color. However, the growing number of black worshipers was something white Methodist el-

Reverend Absalom Jones
From Leon Gardiner Collection, Historical Society of Pennsylvania
Reverend Absalom Jones was one of James Forten's closest friends.

ders were contemplating with disquiet rather than delight, even though they had encouraged Allen to come to St. George's in the first place. When the church was enlarged—with black worshipers helping to pay for the renovations—they were assigned to a remote part of the building. Allen, Jones, and the others made for the "wrong" part of the church that Sunday morning. Pulled from their knees during prayer by two of the white trustees, the four walked out, vowing never to return. It was a dramatic event, and no doubt James Forten heard a lot about it, but he was not there to witness it. While Jones, Allen, and others were drawn to Methodism, he and his family had found *their* religious home at St. Paul's Episcopal Church. The church's evangelical minister, Joseph Pilmore, had proven himself sympathetic to the needs and concerns of his black parishioners and, at least in the early 1790s, James Forten saw no need to abandon St. Paul's.

In time, though, he *would* leave St. Paul's. Just possibly he had become a convert to the idea of a separate black church by 1793. If so, maybe he was present at the roof-raising on August 22, which was marked by a picnic attended by black church members and their white friends and well-wishers like Dr. Rush. Tragically, in a matter of weeks—in some instances a few days—so many of those who had celebrated together would fall victim to yellow fever.

**"A Sunday Morning View of the African Episcopal Church of
St. Thomas in Philadelphia, Taken in June 1829"**
Lithograph by William L. Breton, Historical Society of Pennsylvania
James Forten worshipped in St. Thomas for almost fifty years.

The impact of the epidemic, coupled with a lack of funds, put plans for the church on hold for months, but on July 17, 1794 several hundred people gathered to see the church consecrated. The chances are good that James Forten was there that day, for the church records make it clear that he had, at long last, left St. Paul's and joined what was generally referred to as the African Church. Less than a month after the dedication, the officers of the church set forth their rules. Forten was not one of those officers. Perhaps at age 27 he was considered too young for such an important role. Still, Forten presumably approved of the statement they issued to the public. It was God's will, they explained, that "we would walk in the liberty wherewith Christ has made us free." They named their church St. Thomas's for the "doubting Thomas," who eventually became the first of the disciples to acknowledge the divinity of the risen Christ, and they also put themselves firmly under the jurisdiction of the Protestant Episcopal Church.

The Episcopal bishop, William White, had at first frowned on the notion of a separate black church, but he eventually gave it his blessing. Rebuffed by the Methodists at St. George's, and encouraged by white Episcopalians, most of the members of the African Church decided to affiliate with the Episcopal Church. Perhaps that, as much as anything else, won James Forten over. However, in the short term the decision caused a rift. Neither Allen nor Jones would go along with it. They were Methodists, and Methodists they intended to remain. To objections that the Methodists had cast them out of St. George's they answered that one group of Methodists might have treated them badly, but they believed Methodism was the best faith for "Africans" to follow. Allen remained resolute, but Jones was eventually converted. Allen would go on to establish Mother Bethel, a black church within the Methodist fold, and eventually to found the African Methodist Episcopal denomination. Jones would seek ordination as an Episcopal priest.

On March 28, 1796, Easter Monday, St. Thomas's elected its first vestry, and among the vestrymen was James Forten. Nearing 30, he was now presumably considered old enough for this office. His rise to influence was rapid, and the church became a major focus of his life. Year after year he served on the vestry, advising on all sorts of matters, most of them financial. His growing circle of professional contacts in the white community also put him in a good position when it came to getting legal advice for the church, helping to file for formal incorporation with the Commonwealth of Pennsylvania, and dealing with any number of other issues in the day-to-day running of the church.

In 1801 he was elected president of the Friendly Society of St. Thomas's. Established sometime between 1794 and 1797, the Friendly Society took over from the Free African Society. Each month members paid a quarter into the common fund. The Society would draw on that fund to aid its sick and needy members, bury any whose families were too poor to pay for a decent funeral, and help support deceased members' widows and orphans. Being chosen the Society's president was an unmistakable sign of James Forten's standing within the church. By then, though, he had already achieved recognition in another organization at the heart of African American community life.

What attracted James Forten to Freemasonry? On one level it was those very same things that appealed to others in the Masonic Brotherhood regardless of race—an appreciation of sound morality and religious principles, a love of learning, a sense that men of good repute should band together for the common good, and a desire for fellowship. It was those same goals and values that had brought into the Brotherhood so many of the Founding Fathers, chief among them George Washington.

Brother Washington and Brother Forten would have seen in Freemasonry many of the same things, but for Forten and other aspiring black Masons there were even more attractions. To be a Freemason was to be a *free* Mason, a man whose liberty was recognized. There was also the implied union that came with membership in the fraternity—union with black Masonic brothers in other communities and with white Masons, who would surely extend the hand of friendship to a fellow Mason, whatever the color of his skin. Sadly, as James Forten and his Brothers soon learned, cooperation among black Masons was more easily achieved than a bonding across racial lines.

In their bid to start their own Lodge, the Philadelphians looked to the African Masons in Boston for help. Prince Hall and a number of friends from Boston's small but vibrant free black community had been meeting since the early 1770s and had been formally incorporated into a Lodge by a British military Lodge. Ironically, the men in the British Lodge were soldiers sent over to keep the unruly people of Boston in check, and the African Lodge came into being in the spring of 1775, just before the clashes at Lexington and Concord. Hall and most of his associates were Patriots. At the war's end, and supposedly after being turned down by a white American Lodge for a formal warrant, Hall and the African Masons applied to Britain and got their warrant.

Meanwhile, Philadelphia's black Masons were trying to organize themselves, and they turned to Prince Hall for advice. They explained the problems they had encountered. "The White Masons here say they are afraid to grant us a warrant for fear the black men liv[ing] in Virginia would get to be free masons too." Even if the white Masons had a change of heart, "we had rather be under our Dear Brethren in Boston." Hall promised to help them, and he was true to his word.

There is nothing to indicate when exactly James Forten became a Mason, but by December 27, 1797, the feast of St. John the Evangelist and a day of celebration for Freemasons, he was a Brother in good standing in the Philadelphia African Lodge. Over the next few years the Lodge's minutes are full of the doings of Brother Forten. Not surprisingly, he concerned himself with the Lodge's financial stability, everything from balancing the books to paying the rent on the hall where the Lodge met. He was resourceful and imaginative. Collecting unpaid dues involved tracking down delinquent members and listening to all sorts of excuses. Brothers were reluctant to take on the task—until Forten came up with a tempting arrangement. He proposed that Brethren get a percentage of everything they collected. Two men immediately stepped forward. Clearly, James Forten understood that a cash incentive could make a distasteful job far more appealing.

Besides dealing with financial matters, James Forten took an active part in the other business of the Lodge, investigating applicants for admission, giving a St. John's Day oration on the principles of Masonry, and, as one of the most literate Brethren, writing letters on behalf of the Lodge. The Masons embodied principles he sincerely believed in—devotion to religion, respect for learning, and the practice of charity, since supporting the families of deceased Brothers was one of the prime duties of every Lodge. A bachelor at this point—he did not marry until 1803—Forten found a network of friends among his Brothers in the Lodge.

It was a sad fact that although he found many friends within the Lodge, neither he nor any of his Brothers had much contact with white Masons. The white Lodges of Philadelphia were generally not prepared to accept black Masons as Brothers. A few white Masons did defy the ban on attending meetings of the African Lodge, and now and again—for instance when the different Lodges assembled to pay tribute to George Washington following his death in 1799—the African Lodge was included in Masonic observances. The invitations to participate were always appreciated, but they were rare enough that they were deemed worthy of mention in the African Lodge's official minutes. Brotherhood, it seemed, could not transcend the lines of race—at least as far as most white Masons were concerned.

How long did James Forten remain active in the African Lodge?

We don't know for sure because the records for the years 1801 to 1813 have not survived. By 1813 he had withdrawn from the Lodge, possibly because marriage, children (he had five by 1813) and his growing business demanded too much of his time. However, he remained on good terms with his Masonic Brothers, foremost among them his much-loved and respected minister Absalom Jones, who was the Lodge's Master for years.

The decade and a half from 1785 to 1800 was one of the most momentous periods in James Forten's life. He moved from apprentice to master craftsman. However, he had a life beyond the sailloft. He was drawn increasingly into the growing community of "Africans." Wealth and status—at least in the eyes of whites—did not isolate or insulate him. In part that was because, for all his prosperity, he would never be white. In large part it was because he did not want to be. He was the great-grandson of an African. He knew it and was proud of it. But he was an American too, and he had fought to create the country he felt instinctively was his. What James Forten was working out for himself—his identity as a person of African descent in America—was what every member of his community was working out. Beyond the black community, it was also what Americans of European ancestry were working out. Could the United States, founded on a promise of equality, live up to that promise? James Forten and the other black men and women in what was, at least for a time, the new nation's capital city, hoped it could. In the decades that followed, though, that optimism would be put to the test, and James Forten would have to grapple with the question of whether an "African" could ever truly be an "American."

CHAPTER ELEVEN

"A Man of Colour" Speaks Out

By 1800 James Forten had not only become a business owner; he had established himself as a man of influence within Philadelphia's free black community. Over the next decade and a half he would build on those foundations. His increasing prosperity and business know-how contributed to his standing. Here was a man with the knowledge and the means to get things done. As the years passed, he assumed a larger and larger role in defending black Philadelphians, himself included, from hostile laws, harassment, and open violence.

To get a sense of James Forten's activism after 1800 we need to step back for a moment to the 1790s when he was just beginning to make his presence felt. The year 1793 was filled with social and political turmoil. It was also the year when the deadly yellow fever struck. For black people that same year saw yet another cause for anxiety. Congress passed the Fugitive Slave Law. When they learned what it meant in everyday terms, African Americans were deeply afraid. It meant escaped slaves could be seized and returned to bondage. It also made kidnapping fairly easy. Willing to commit perjury and swear that the black person in custody was the same "boy" or "wench" who had run away years before, a claimant could carry off into slavery a freeborn man or woman.

The leaders of the African American community and their white friends in the Pennsylvania Abolition Society petitioned many times in the 1790s for the repeal of the law, the freeing of all of Pennsylvania's remaining slaves, and, as a long-range goal, the outlawing of slavery throughout the United States. Every approach to the state or Federal government was rebuffed. Refusing to give up, in 1799 black Philadelphians launched yet another assault on slavery in general and the Fugitive Slave Law in particular. Absalom Jones and some seventy other men of color submitted a petition to Congress. In the short term they wanted action to stop the wholesale kidnapping that was going on under cover of the Fugitive Slave Law. They pointed out, however, that kidnapping would only cease when black people were no longer considered "property" anywhere in the United States. They longed to see slavery ended. They knew that was not going to happen overnight, but their second request was that Congress should at least "prepare the way for the oppressed to go free."

When the petition was presented to Congress in January 1800, members from both the North and the South were appalled. Who did "Africans" think they were to approach Congress? Were they planning a rebellion? Did they want the right to vote, or even run for office? Surely they were too ignorant to have written the petition themselves. White men, probably that interfering bunch from the Pennsylvania Abolition Society, had written it for them.

A few members were mildly sympathetic, but only one believed the petition should be debated. George Thacher of Massachusetts was a Harvard-trained lawyer and an outspoken foe of slavery. He considered the petition respectful and worthy of consideration, and he outraged his colleagues by comparing slavery to a deadly cancer eating away at the heart of the new nation. Alas, his was a lone voice calling for justice.

James Forten followed the progress of the petition with intense interest; and, when it was thrown out, he sent Thacher a letter of thanks for his commitment to the cause of liberty. The letter was widely reprinted in the press, not only in Philadelphia but throughout the North and the Upper South, and it is easy to see why. It was eloquent and heartfelt. Forten wanted Thacher to know how much his efforts were appreciated by "Africans and descendants of that unhappy race" across the nation, for the petition had been sent to Congress on behalf of them all, free and enslaved. And no, they had no intention of resorting to violence, as some members of Congress had charged. They hoped for peaceful change and a rewriting of the nation's laws to free the enslaved and raise the entire black community to equality and full citizenship. "Though our faces are black, yet we are men, and though many among us cannot write because our rulers have thought [it] proper to keep us in ignorance, yet we...have the feelings and the passions of men [and] are as anxious to enjoy the birthright" of all Americans, namely liberty. With the rejection of their petition, "A deep gloom now envelopes us," relieved only by the knowledge that "there is one who will use all his endeavors to free the Slaves...and preserve the Free Black in the full enjoyment of his rights."

In his letter James Forten emphasized the essential equality of all Americans and the need for a sweeping but non-violent transformation of society. In 1801 he took his argument several steps further. Through the 1790s the Pennsylvania Abolition Society had been reaching out to Philadelphia's free black people, trying to secure for them employment, education, and protection from oppression. Members visited people's homes, spoke to community groups, and issued circulars full of well-meant (if to our ears rather patronizing) advice. In 1801 the PAS prepared yet another address and sent copies to, among others, the Friendly Society of St. Thomas. On behalf of the society its president, James Forten, wrote to express their gratitude to the PAS for its help, especially in promoting education. It was education that would "remove the prejudices against us" and "raise the African race to the rank of Man in the Creation."

Fighting ignorance was one of James Forten's major goals. In a sense, it was his *only* goal. Dispel ignorance, and the nation would indeed live up to the principles enshrined in the Declaration of Independence. That goal of rooting out ignorance explained his devotion to Freemasonry, with its pursuit of spiritual enlightenment. It explained his determination to see black children and adults given the benefits of education. And it explained his desire to reach out to hostile whites. Once let light break in upon *their* ignorance, and the result would be not only the abolition of slavery but the creation of a society from which prejudice and injustice would be banished forever.

Enlightenment took many forms, and James Forten was happy to work with anyone who shared his aspirations. He was intrigued in 1801 when local printer William W. Woodward brought around a subscription paper. Woodward wanted to publish in one bound volume an antislavery novel, the Marquis de Bois-Robert's *The Negro Equaled by Few Europeans,* and selected poems of the African-born poet Phillis Wheatley. There was nothing unusual in soliciting advance orders. Publishers routinely did so to be sure a book would sell before they risked too much of their own money. However, in a departure from established practice, Woodward approached both black and white readers. James Forten signed up to buy a copy, as did a number of other black Philadelphians. They could spare a dollar for a worthy cause. Let their willingness to support intellectual endeavors stand alongside the work of the African poet and the Frenchman's condemnation of slavery and racial prejudice.

Ignorance proved difficult to dispel, though, as James Forten soon discovered. In 1804 white Philadelphians were outraged by reports that, following the July Fourth celebrations, gangs of young black men had been roaming around attacking and robbing whites and threatening large-scale violence. The reports were rather vague—the number of perpetrators leaped from a handful to several dozen and then to a couple of hundred—but they led to immediate demands for action. Some citizens wanted to tax all free people for the support of their poor. Others called for laws to stop any more black people settling in Pennsylvania, the harsh punishment of black vagrants, and lengthy prison terms for black lawbreakers. The image of African Americans as lazy and addicted to crime was growing.

James Forten and others in the emerging black middle class responded in various ways. They promoted education, urged tough punishments for any lawbreakers, regardless of race, and tried to show that there were many African Americans who were hardworking and law-abiding. The same year as the July Fourth unrest, Forten's church achieved its long-cherished goal of opening a school, and James Forten became one of its trustees. In 1809, with the warm approval of a number of prominent whites, the members of St. Thomas's Church organized the Society for the Suppression of Vice and Immorality. Needless to say, James Forten was involved in the work of the society.

Try as they might, Forten and other men of influence within the black community could not stem the rising tide of racial hostility. Violence against their persons and their institutions, especially their churches, was a fact of life. A foreign visitor was shocked at the "liberties taken in the public streets, where boys of ten or twelve…seem to think, that they are privileged in insulting this unfortunate class of our fellow-beings almost indiscriminately," while adults looked on and approved.

A host of factors came together to make Philadelphia a less welcoming place for black people in the 1800s than it had been in the 1790s—and life had been tough back then. In the first decade of the new century the economy fluctuated wildly. Thrown out of work, or fearful they soon would be, whites took out their frustrations on their black neighbors. The city was under pressure. White immigrants were flooding in, as were black people from the Upper South. Wave upon wave of black Southerners fled north to Philadelphia, the first large city they came to after crossing the Mason-Dixon Line. Some thrived in this new setting, but many did not. Poverty-stricken and in a more desperate situation than the black migrants of the 1790s, these men and women were more likely to seek relief at the almshouse, beg in the streets, or fall foul of the law. White citizens demanded action from the authorities to curb the influx, and for good measure they included in those demands restrictions on the freedom of long-term black residents.

Despite the growing racial antagonism in the city, James Forten found reason to be hopeful. The black community was not without white friends. The Pennsylvania Abolition Society was still working to end slavery and see that free people of color were protected in the enjoyment of their rights. During the 1800s James Forten developed close ties with a number of the most dedicated individuals in the PAS.

By 1807 James Forten believed he saw signs that the federal government was at long last moving in the right direction. A bill outlawing the slave trade passed the House and Senate and was signed into law by President Jefferson. As of January 1, 1808, no more slaves could be imported into the United States. Since Britain had announced a similar ban, this looked like the beginning of the end. Once the trade in slaves ceased, Forten and his allies reasoned, the abolition of slavery could not be far behind. It did not occur to them that some congressmen from the Upper South supported the ban on imports because it meant they and their constituents could get better prices for their own slaves when they sold the ones they did not want to planters in the new cotton-producing states further to the south.

Unaware of any hidden agenda, black Philadelphians believed the end of the slave trade was something worth celebrating, as did members of other African American communities throughout the North. James Forten and other representatives of black churches and mutual benefit societies began planning a day of thanksgiving. Nothing short of a catastrophe could have kept James Forten away from St. Thomas's Church on January 1, 1808, where he heard Rev. Absalom Jones preach a sermon beginning, fittingly enough, with a verse from Exodus.

James Forten probably helped organize the January 1st observances in following years and spent a good part of each New Year's Day in church giving thanks for the abolition of the slave trade. In 1812 the orator was his friend, printer Russell Parrott. In 1814 and 1816 Parrott was again the speaker. In 1818 one of the sponsoring groups was Forten's own Friendly Society of St. Thomas. On two occasions the speakers were sons of a man he held in the highest esteem. Like their father, John Gloucester Sr., Jeremiah and John Jr. were Presbyterian ministers. Like their father, both had been born into slavery. Listening to these eloquent young men, Forten could feel something like paternal pride, for he had helped John Sr. raise the money to buy their freedom. The January 1st orations were always worth listening to, but as the years passed and the end of the slave trade was *not* followed by the end of slavery, James Forten's optimism started to fade.

In the summer of 1812 the United States stumbled and lurched into a second war with Britain. In common with most Northern businessmen, James Forten was less than enthusiastic about the war. He may even have shared in the grim predictions of disaster.

As the Revolutionary War had done, the War of 1812 would test his sense of himself as an American. However, it would do so in a way very different from that earlier conflict.

"Independence Day Celebration in Centre Square, Philadelphia"
By John Lewis Krimmel, 1819
As James Forten lamented, although African Americans
had fought in the struggle for independence, they were less
and less welcome at the annual July Fourth celebrations.

This second war with Britain would not be marked by many American victories, at least in its early stages, but James Forten, ever the patriot, joined in celebrating those victories that *were* achieved. On August 19, 1812, some 750 miles out in the Atlantic, Isaac Hull's *Constitution* forced the surrender of the Royal Navy frigate *Guerrière*. When news of this triumph over British sea power reached Philadelphia, the citizens were ecstatic, and none more so than James Forten, who donated ten dollars to a collection to buy gifts for Captain Hull and his first lieutenant. It was an acknowledgement of victory, and it was also a celebration of belonging. Forten was sharing in "the Glory acquired for our Country." However, his buoyant mood would be short-lived.

In the early months of the war there were renewed calls for restrictions on Pennsylvania's black population. Many white citizens were becoming increasingly frustrated at the failure of lawmakers to ban black migration into the state and keep a tight rein on long-term black residents. By 1813 legislators were being deluged with calls to do something, *anything*, about the number of black people in the state. An anonymous writer to one Philadelphia newspaper even suggested using African Americans as cannon-fodder on the battlefield, reasoning that if enough of them were killed it would solve the over-population problem!

On January 18, 1813 the Pennsylvania House appointed a committee to consider closing the state's borders to black migrants. Plenty of whites liked what they heard and urged lawmakers to go further. Black people should be registered and a special tax imposed upon them. Black felons should be sold for a period of time into what amounted to slavery. Demands for harsh new laws came in every day. James Forten knew he had to respond. The pamphlet he produced, *Letters from a Man of Colour,* was and remains a bold and persuasive appeal to justice and common sense.

James Forten described his reflections as "the simple dictates of nature" and insisted his letters "are not written in the gorgeous style of a scholar, nor dressed in…literary perfection." Nevertheless, his pamphlet indicates how well-read he was. He prefaced his appeal with four lines of verse from the work of the eighteenth-century English essayist Joseph Addison on the beauty of liberty. He went on to remind his readers what the Founding Fathers had said—sentiments he feared many white Americans were now trying to ignore. "We hold this truth to be self-evident, that GOD created all men equal, and [it] is one of the most prominent features in the Declaration of Independence and in that glorious fabric of collected wisdom, our noble Constitution." He insisted that "this truth" applied to everyone, regardless of race. The bill to which he so strenuously objected had failed in the Pennsylvania Senate, but he had learned it was to be held over to the next session. He wanted to make sure it died.

The regrettable fact that "there are a number of worthless men belonging to our color" should not blind lawmakers to the merits of the black community as a whole. Surely African Americans had earned the right to equal treatment. "Many of our ancestors were brought here more than one hundred years ago; many of our fathers, many of ourselves, have fought and bled for the Independence of our country."

He refused to believe that the white men of the Revolutionary generation had been hypocrites. "They knew we were deeper skinned than they were, but they acknowledged us as men, and found that many an honest heart beat beneath a dusky bosom. They felt that they had no more authority to enslave us, than England had to tyrannize over them." Those early lawmakers whom he praised as "patriotic citizens" had written a constitution for the Commonwealth of Pennsylvania that declared: "All men are born equally free and independent." Now it seemed that a new generation of lawmakers was denying the basic humanity of black Pennsylvanians. "[W]hy are we not to be considered as men? Has the GOD who made the white man and the black, left any record declaring us a separate species?"

The bill was riddled with "evils…fatal to the rights of freemen, and…characteristic of European despotism." If a black family received a visit from a friend from out of state, they must report that friend's presence within twenty-four hours or pay a hefty fine. They themselves must register with the local authorities. And how would they be expected to show that they had complied with the law? Must they wear a collar? And must they register their children within twenty-four hours of their birth? "What have the people of Colour been guilty of" that they should be subjected to such treatment, he demanded to know.

One of the worst features of the proposed law, according to Forten, was that it would give free rein to those who already considered black people "little above the brute creation." Drawing on personal observation and experience, he sketched a scenario in which the Constable could transform the business of law enforcement into sport. He could single out a black man in the street and demand to see his certificate of registration. If the man fled, the Constable could "raise the boys in hue and cry against" him. The unfortunate man would be chased down, hustled away in shackles, imprisoned until an "owner" appeared, and if none appeared— because he was a free man and had none—he could be sold for seven years. Contemplating this, James Forten could barely contain his sense of outrage. "My God, what a situation is his. Search the legends of tyranny and find no precedent."

He ended with an admission that "My feelings are acute." If his eloquence was insufficient to produce the desired result, "I trust the eloquence of nature will succeed, and that the law-givers of this happy Commonwealth will yet remain the Blacks' friend[s]." If he hoped to change white hearts and minds, he was sadly disappointed. The legislative package failed largely because it was unworkable, but the calls for restrictions continued. In a matter of months, however, lawmakers had a crisis of truly alarming proportions to cope with, and it pushed everything else into the background.

The struggle with Britain had gone badly. Shortages of men and materiel offset most of the gains America's forces made. By the summer of 1814 Britain had freed herself from the conflict with Napoleon in Europe and was concentrating her full might against the United States. On August 24 Washington, D.C. fell to a well-planned

British assault. Philadelphians feared their city would be next. On the morning of August 26 James Forten left his sail-loft to attend a hastily convened meeting in the State House Yard to discuss how best to defend Philadelphia. It was decided that the city's first line of defense should be a huge earthwork along the Schuylkill River. Since no troops could be spared for this massive construction project, the work must be done by civilian volunteers. Various groups stepped forward, including the city's men of color, and at their head was none other than James Forten.

Aided by Russell Parrott and ministers Absalom Jones and Richard Allen, who read from their pulpits the call for volunteers, James Forten gathered the names of those willing to labor on the fortifications, and the city's Committee of Defense set aside September 21 as *their* day. The black volunteers, some two and a half thousand of them, met at dawn and marched to Gray's Ferry, where they labored until nightfall. James Forten marshaled his black employees and toiled alongside them. In the end, the British did not attack Philadelphia, but black residents, Forten among them, had made their point. They would stand shoulder-to-shoulder with white residents and defend the city they all called home.

Eager though he was to prove his patriotism, James Forten longed for peace. On February 15, 1815 he wrote his friend Paul Cuffe in Massachusetts with the news they had both been waiting for. Couriers had just arrived from Washington with word that the Senate had ratified the Treaty of Ghent. The war was over, and at least in Philadelphia people were celebrating in the streets.

The war's end paved the way for the revival of an undertaking dear to the hearts of Cuffe and Forten. For Paul Cuffe it would see a cherished dream move closer to realization. For James Forten it would prove an exercise in frustration. *His* dream would turn into something more akin to a nightmare.

CHAPTER TWELVE

Captain Cuffe's Plan

Long before Paul Cuffe spoke to him about it, James Forten was aware of plans to resettle black people from the British Empire in the West African colony of Sierra Leone. It had been talked about in England when he was there. If he had not heard about it then, he would certainly have heard about it after he returned to Philadelphia because it was under discussion by, among others, members of the Free African Society.

In time the colony absorbed some of the African American men who had fought for Britain during the Revolution. It became home to hundreds of Jamaican maroons—rebellious runaway slaves who made their peace with the British and agreed to be shipped from the West Indies to a new home in Africa. Sierra Leone was also the place to which Royal Navy ships took people rescued from illegal slavers after Britain banned the slave trade. The colony had its problems, and in 1807 the British government took it over from the privately-run Sierra Leone Company. A group of philanthropists formed the African Institution and helped oversee the colony. They were interested in seeing Sierra Leone make money, but more important to them was ending slavery by suppressing the slave trade and spreading Christianity in Africa. Such talk interested Quaker reformers on both sides of the Atlantic, including Paul Cuffe. In time he would recruit James Forten.

White Americans who heard about Paul Cuffe and James Forten often made the mistake of thinking of them as virtually identical. Both were men of African descent and both made their living from the sea, Forten as a sailmaker and Cuffe as a ship-owner and sea-captain. However, there were significant differences between them, and those differences shaped their views of the world around them. Cuffe had been born on a tiny island off the Massachusetts coast, and had spent his early years there before moving to the community of Westport, close to New Bedford. His father was West African and his mother Native American. Forten had obviously had a very different childhood. As for his ties to Africa, they were less direct than Cuffe's. Forten knew his great-grandfather was an African, but pin-pointing a precise place on the vast continent of Africa and a people from whom he could trace his descent was impossible. Then there was the matter of religion. Cuffe was a convert to Quakerism, and Forten was a lifelong Episcopalian.

Despite their differences, a close bond developed between the two men. Cuffe was often in Philadelphia on business or to converse with his fellow Quakers in the city that was the hub of American Quakerism. The sails on one or other of his ships always needed repairing, and it was only a matter of time before his search for a competent sailmaker took him to James Forten's loft. Through his new friend, Cuffe met other prominent men in the city's growing free black community. In return, Cuffe introduced James Forten to some of Philadelphia's Quaker merchants and, since quite a few of them were ship-owners, that was good for business.

In December 1807 Paul Cuffe made one of his regular trips to Philadelphia. While he was in town he heard from white abolitionists, many of them Quakers, about Sierra Leone and the African

Institution. He almost certainly discussed with James Forten the possibility of trading with the African colony. Neither man was opposed to making money, and if that could be combined with serving a good cause, so much the better.

Cuffe was eager to investigate things for himself, but there was a problem. Tensions were heating up between the United States and Britain, so trading with, or even visiting a British colony was not easy. While he waited for the situation to improve, Cuffe began writing to British abolitionists, and in the letters back and forth James Forten's name started to surface as Cuffe told his correspondents about his friend and mentioned his talent for business.

Captain Paul Cuffe
Captain Cuffe was one of James Forten's closest friends.

Toward the end of 1810 Cuffe was finally able to make a voyage to Sierra Leone. He set sail from Philadelphia just after Christmas on his ship the *Traveller*. Once in the colony, he started talking with people—the governor, the settlers, and the local people. He liked what he saw and heard, and from Sierra Leone he headed to England to meet with government officials and members of the African Institution. He was able to report back to James Forten and other friends that his meetings had gone well, and he was optimistic as he sailed home. At this point he was thinking about trade between the United States and Sierra Leone, and just possibly taking over to the colony a few settlers.

An unpleasant surprise awaited him upon his return. Things had become so bad between the United States and Britain that trade between the two countries had been virtually outlawed. Cuffe did not know that. He had British goods on board the *Traveller*. Customs officials seized his ship, but he made the best of a bad situation. He got letters from several influential white friends and boarded a stagecoach bound for the nation's capital to plead his case. His efforts paid off, and he got his ship back.

On his way home from Washington, Cuffe spent a couple of days in Baltimore meeting with black and white abolitionists, and then he moved on to Philadelphia. There he called on some of his Quaker friends, on members of the Pennsylvania Abolition Society, and on prominent people of color, including, of course, James Forten. Cuffe told them about Sierra Leone and urged them to begin writing to people in the colony, as well as to the African Institution. After saying farewell to Forten and his other Philadelphia acquaintances, Cuffe went to New York, where he paid a similar round of visits.

Soon after he returned to Westport, Cuffe received a letter from two of the officers of the African Institution. They promised him land in Sierra Leone and said they hoped he would move there.

Whether or not he decided to relocate, they encouraged him to bring over from the United States a few free black families who had money and marketable skills.

The outbreak of the War of 1812 put plans on hold. Although Paul Cuffe tried to get Congress to give him the go-ahead to trade with the British colony, arguing that his was purely a humanitarian mission, his petition was turned down. He was frustrated, but he refused to give up hope. He would just have to be patient.

Meanwhile, James Forten and Paul Cuffe were still in touch with one another, swapping ideas and updating one another on steps they had taken or ideas for the future. As the ink dried on the peace treaty between Britain and the United States, Cuffe put forward an intriguing suggestion. Why didn't Forten and other prosperous black people pool their money and build a ship for the African trade? Forten was interested. If they had a ship, he knew who would be making her sails.

As soon as peace was restored, Cuffe started preparing for his second voyage to Sierra Leone. At Cuffe's urging, Forten and his good friend Russell Parrott began recruiting people to go to the colony with him. They located two couples, Antoine and Elizabeth Servance and Samuel and Barbery Wilson. Both of the men had been born in West Africa, and they leaped at the chance to return home. Cuffe thought highly of all four when he met them. He was particularly impressed by Antoine Servance, who could read, write, and do mathematics, and proudly declared that he considered himself inferior to no man, white or black.

In the fall of 1815 James Forten reported to Cuffe that he was receiving all sorts of inquiries about the African venture—from prospective emigrants, from people who wanted to trade with the colony, and so on. He and Parrott also took the initiative and sent a letter to the African Institution. They explained the steps they had already taken, and they mentioned the kinds of people they had recruited—respectable people with useful skills. They also asked about incentives the British government was prepared to offer them and their friends to promote trade with Sierra Leone. Whatever else Forten and Parrott had in mind, they hoped to turn a profit from the African enterprise.

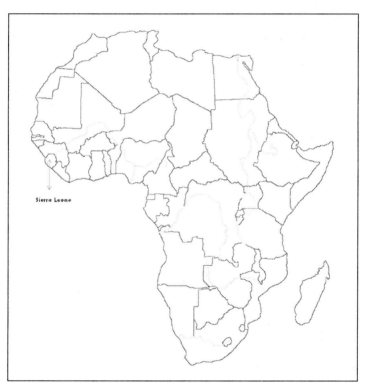

Africa Showing Location of Sierra Leone.

Meanwhile, Paul Cuffe had been corresponding with a white minister, Samuel J. Mills. The minister had first contacted Cuffe in 1814 to say that he had been considering setting up a colony for free black people—a place where they could live apart from whites, and perhaps a first step towards abolishing slavery in the United States. Mills had been thinking about the American West now that the United States had acquired the vast Louisiana Territory. Cuffe had written back that he was more interested in Africa. This marked the start of a regular correspondence between the two men. Shortly before Cuffe's second voyage to Sierra Leone, Rev. Mills wrote him that growing numbers of white people in the United States were turning their attention to Africa and the plight of her scattered children. Cuffe was delighted. Although he was not yet preaching the idea of a mass exodus, he was moving in that direction.

The *Traveller* left for Africa from Westport in December 1815. On board were thirty-eight emigrants, including the four Forten and Parrott had recruited. The crossing was a rough one, but the vessel and her passengers and crew made it safely to Sierra Leone. However, no sooner had Cuffe set foot on dry land than he found himself caught up in a tangle of red tape. His commercial license from the British government had not arrived, and the governor took some persuading before he would let Cuffe sell his trade goods. Obviously there were issues that had to be hammered out before Cuffe could think of making another voyage to the colony. Still, he hoped for the best.

Once Cuffe returned home he put his friends to work recruiting more emigrants. James Forten's assignment was to find a watch repairer, a man who understood how to build and operate a rice mill, and another who could get a saw-mill up and running. And for the first time Cuffe began talking about resettling large numbers of black people from the United States in Africa. He speculated that it might be a way of preventing the kind of bloodshed that had occurred on Saint Domingue. As he told Rev. Mills, slaveowners could only do away with their fears of rebellion if they freed their slaves. And if they were hesitant to act because they did not like the idea of living alongside their former slaves, then something must be done to address that issue. To achieve a good thing, namely the ending of slavery, perhaps there should be a separate colony for black people.

Apparently other white men besides Rev. Mills agreed with Cuffe. In December 1816, from his lodgings in the nation's capital, Robert Finley, a Presbyterian minister from New Jersey, sent a letter to Cuffe. Finley had heard a lot about Cuffe and hoped to interest him in a scheme *he* had been working on. He described how distressed he and other whites were about the plight of free black people in the Northern states. So many were poor and seemed to have no future in America. If those he described as "the more virtuous and industrious" agreed to emigrate, they would improve their own prospects and help "civilize" (his term) Africa. Would Cuffe assist him in this worthy undertaking?

Cuffe wrote back to say that he was interested, but he warned that the British would probably not welcome an influx of black Americans into Sierra Leone. Perhaps a separate American-sponsored colony should be established in Africa, and for good measure perhaps there should be a second colony on America's western frontier for those who did not like the idea of a long and hazardous trans-Atlantic voyage.

If Paul Cuffe had read the pamphlet Finley was writing, he might have been less encouraging. In *Thoughts on the Colonization of Free Blacks* Finley urged that slavery be abolished, but only if black people agreed to leave the United States. He feared the creation of a multiracial society and wanted nothing to do with a colony anywhere on the American continent. His motive for traveling to Washington was to interest the rich and the powerful in his project. He was well-connected. His brother-in-law, Elias B. Caldwell, was Clerk of the U.S. Supreme Court. One of Caldwell's friends was influential lawyer (and author of "The Star-Spangled Banner") Francis Scott Key. Through Caldwell and Key, Finley was able to recruit men like Henry Clay, the Speaker of the House of Representatives, and war hero Andrew Jackson, to help him form a society to establish a colony in Africa.

Samuel J. Mills heard what was being planned and hurried to Washington. He arrived in time to attend a preliminary meeting. Paul Cuffe learned in a letter from Mills what was going on, and he wrote back to say how pleased he was. He gave Mills James Forten's name and said he hoped he and other leading members of the various free black communities in the North would be involved in the undertaking.

Within days of the first informal planning meeting in Washington—either at the very end of December 1816 or in the first day or two of the New Year—the American Colonization Society was born. While some of its officers were committed to spreading the Christian faith in Africa and ending slavery, the majority had a rather different agenda. They believed that black people, especially those who were free, must be separated from white people. As for abolishing slavery, they agreed that that was best left vague. After all, a good number of them were slave-owners.

Philadelphians got their first inkling of what was being discussed when reports from Washington newspapers were reprinted in newspapers in their own city. One of the items was an account of Henry Clay's speech on colonization in which he made it clear what he and his friends were thinking. Clay insisted that free blacks had no future in America. He said nothing about freeing the slaves.

By the middle of January, many black Philadelphians were convinced that a plan was being worked out to deport them to Africa. James Forten saw no need for panic. He thought people were overreacting and were misinformed about what was actually going on. Still, he could not ignore a matter he heard being spoken of everywhere—at church, in the street, and in his own sail-loft. Forten did admit in a letter to Cuffe that "the People of Colour here was very much fri[gh]tened." He added that there had been a meeting at Richard Allen's church, Mother Bethel. What he neglected to mention was his role in that meeting. There is nothing in the records to indicate who called that meeting. Perhaps Forten and his allies called it in the belief that they could calm people's fears, or perhaps it simply grew out of the determination of scores of black Philadelphians to present a united front in the face of what they saw as a very grave threat. If the attendance reflected the depth of their concern, they were very worried indeed. Forten estimated that three thousand people crowded into Mother Bethel. He was obliged to tell Cuffe that among that number there was not a single person who wanted to go to Africa.

Although his letter to Cuffe suggested otherwise, James Forten had not stood silently by at the meeting. He seems to have reasoned that, if people wanted to go on record as being opposed to deportation, he could support that. And certainly the resolutions he and Russell Parrott helped draw up were clear enough on *that* point. "WHEREAS our ancestors (not of choice) were the first successful cultivators of America, we...feel ourselves entitled to participate in the blessings of her luxuriant soil." They went on to express their sense of kinship with the slaves. They would not trek off to Africa and abandon their less fortunate brothers and sisters. They would stay and try to liberate them. There was nothing here that represented a radical departure from James Forten's earlier views. He had never favored forced resettlement, and he had always spoken of the moral duty of free people to work for the freedom of the enslaved.

Several days after the Mother Bethel meeting, there was a smaller meeting. Rev. Finley was traveling back from Washington to his home in New Jersey when he passed through Philadelphia. He learned about the Bethel meeting and arranged to get together with prominent members of the black community. He spent the better part of an hour talking with them and, by the end of that time, he felt he had convinced them that the founders of the American Colonization Society were "benevolent and good." As for where exactly the proposed colony should be located, some of the Philadelphians favored the American West and others Africa. According to Finley's biographer, James Forten was particularly vocal. "He said their people would become a great nation," and he pointed to Haiti as proof of that. He declared that Africa was the best place for a colony, saying it would be bad for black people to settle anywhere near whites.

Is that really what James Forten said? It seems unlikely, but then there was a stray comment he made to Cuffe that "they"—did he mean all black people or just some black people—"will never become a people until they come out from amongst the white people." His statements to Cuffe and to Finley suggest he may have been trying to work out for himself what he saw as the future of black people in America—and how he saw his own future.

CHAPTER THIRTEEN

"America Is Our True Home"

Through the spring of 1817 James Forten remained a supporter of the African enterprise. He contacted Cuffe on behalf of a white man, "a Merchant I work for, and a very great friend of mine," who wanted to know more about trade prospects in Sierra Leone. Forten himself was eager to learn "whether you have had any late information from Africa." He had to wait several months for a reply; and when it came, it was not in Cuffe's handwriting. Too sick to hold a pen, he had had to dictate his letter to a family member. Forten hurriedly wrote back. He and his family were distressed that their dear friend was so sick. They were praying for his speedy recovery. Forten offered encouraging words about the African colony. He believed there *must* be a colony. Increasingly, though, he was asking himself whether the American Colonization Society was the right organization to set one up. Just what was its agenda?

Although James Forten and many others in the black community thought of the ACS as a powerful organization, in its early months it met with less success than its founders had hoped. They asked Congress for help in establishing a colony in Africa, but the answer they got was that the ACS should take to Sierra Leone any emigrants it could round up. Refusing to give up, the men in the inner circle of the ACS decided to send someone to West Africa to report back on the best site for an American-sponsored colony. But paying the expenses of an agent would cost money, and so the ACS launched a fund-raising campaign. In the summer of 1817 the push began to create an auxiliary in Philadelphia. At a "whites only" meeting at City Hall on August 6, some in the audience questioned whether colonization would really hasten the freeing of the slaves in the South. Unhappy with the answers they got, they walked out, but enough people remained behind to organize a Philadelphia branch of the ACS, and that stirred up fears on the part of many in the black community. By now James Forten was among their number.

On August 10, just four days after the founding of the Philadelphia auxiliary, Forten chaired a protest meeting. He and Russell Parrott drew up an address *To the humane and benevolent Inhabitants of the city and county of Philadelphia*—the very people the ACS was trying to enlist. They insisted that free blacks did not want to be colonized—at least not as the ACS proposed to colonize them. As for the argument that colonization would hasten the end of slavery, that was false. Planters would ship off to Africa the more independent-minded of their slaves, while holding on to "the tame and submissive" and treating them even worse than before.

Despite his growing hostility to the ACS, James Forten had been careful not to denounce all emigration plans. If the ACS was made up of deceitful men intent on propping up the institution of slavery by deporting free people, the same could not be said of the African Institution. But Forten's link with the African Institution was Paul Cuffe, and Cuffe was ominously silent. As the weeks passed, Forten grew increasingly worried. Finally a letter came with the news he had feared: his old friend was dead.

Other deaths followed in rapid succession. Robert Finley took a teaching position in Georgia and succumbed to malaria. Samuel J. Mills went to West Africa to inspect sites for a colony, fell ill on his way home, died of fever, and was buried at sea. The American Colonization Society survived, though, and it pushed ahead with its plans for a colony. It found itself facing an uphill battle when it came to getting settlers. While its officers might reject as baseless rumors that all free black people in the United States were to be rounded up and forced into exile, the damage had been done. One of those who could not be convinced to endorse the ACS was James Forten. While at first he had insisted that the society was made up of good men with good intentions, he had come at last to share the views of the majority of black Philadelphians: the ACS was evil, and he and they wanted nothing to do with it.

With James Forten now spearheading their efforts, black Philadelphians continued their attacks. On November 16, 1819, Forten and Parrott presided over a meeting called to respond to an address from the ACS to people of color in New York and Philadelphia. They insisted that black Philadelphians had already stated their opposition to the ACS clearly and forcefully, and nothing had happened to make them change their minds. The insistence of the ACS leadership that the society did not intend to interfere with slavery only deepened their hatred of the organization. Yes, the ACS had made some black converts, but while "a few obscure and dissatisfied strangers among us" might dream of becoming "presidents, governors and principals in Africa," the Philadelphians wanted the ACS to be in no doubt that "there is but one sentiment among the respectable inhabitants of color…which is, that it meets [with] their unanimous and decided disapprobation."

A few weeks later, a Philadelphia newspaper printed a letter from James Forten written under an alias he had used before, "A Man of Colour." He began with a statement on a subject close to his heart—liberty. It was sacred—"a right which God has bestowed on all."

The colonization scheme was "calculated to perpetuate Slavery in this Land of Liberty." The supposedly benevolent gentlemen who put forward the idea of a colony had not yet decided whether to locate it in Africa or the North American wilderness. He wanted them to know that he wouldn't go to either place, and neither would the vast majority of free black people. They intended to stay put and push for all the rights they were entitled to as American citizens.

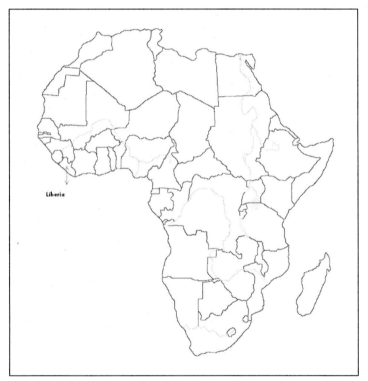

Africa Showing Location of Liberia

Over the next few years James Forten and other opponents of colonization had reason to be worried. Despite serious financial problems, the American Colonization Society did not fade away. It managed to find allies in Congress and in the White House, and it got help to found a colony in West Africa. The first shipload of people left from New York on the *Elizabeth* in 1820. Some were freeborn and believed their prospects would be brighter in Africa, but the majority had had little choice in the matter. They were slaves who had been freed on the condition that they agree to go to Africa.

The *Elizabeth* sailed with what amounted to a naval escort. The U. S. Navy squadron was to look for a place on the West African coast to set up a base from which to hunt down illegal slavers now that the United States had officially withdrawn from the trans-Atlantic slave trade. If the emigrants wanted to live at that base, they were of course welcome to do so. The United States government wanted to play down any suggestion that it was setting up a colony. This was a private undertaking...although it was most certainly one that had a lot of government help.

Even though the ACS had powerful backers in the United States, including President James Monroe, its first expedition was very nearly its last. Negotiations with African rulers for land went nowhere. As for the unfortunate settlers from the *Elizabeth*, most took refuge in Sierra Leone, where they died in droves from malaria. Bright promises of freedom and financial independence in Africa led many to their deaths.

Despite the dreadful losses among the people on the *Elizabeth*, further expeditions were dispatched, and inevitably there were more deaths. Other issues arose. Vastly exceeding his orders, U. S. Navy Lieutenant Robert Field Stockton, who had gone over with the first group of settlers, entered into the bargaining for land. Putting a loaded pistol to the head of King Peter, who controlled the region to the south of Sierra Leone that the Colonization Society wanted to buy, Stockton told him to accept the terms the Americans were offering or he would blow his brains out! Needless to say, Stockton's action produced a legacy of distrust and hostility. The ACS had its colony, and it began settling its emigrants there, but by the end of 1822 they found themselves fighting for their lives, not only against "African fever" but against a coalition of forces from various local peoples. Although a truce was eventually worked out, it was an uneasy truce. There were also tensions between the emigrants and the white agents sent over to govern them.

Back in the United States, James Forten was well placed to receive graphic accounts of the suffering of the settlers. As a sailmaker, he counted many seafaring men among his friends. Some had been to West Africa, and they told him about the situation there. He heard about the desperate plight of the settlers in Liberia, as the American colony was now called. Tales of deaths from disease and deaths from clashes with the local peoples only strengthened his conviction that the ACS must be stopped before it did even more harm.

The ACS kept boasting of finding scores of recruits in Philadelphia. While Forten and others questioned the numbers, they did have to admit that economic hard times, combined with pervasive racism, made Liberia look more appealing to some people than an uncertain future in the City of Brotherly Love. And one of the people lured by the ACS's promises was a member of James Forten's own workforce.

Born into slavery in South Carolina, Francis Devany had gained his freedom and moved to Philadelphia, where he had found work in the Forten sail-loft. Convinced he could do even better in Liberia, in 1823 he decided to emigrate with his family. He did do well in the colony, earning enough to set himself up as a trader in the Liberian capital of Monrovia, named in honor of ACS well-wisher President Monroe. In less than six years Devany was worth between fifteen and twenty thousand dollars. Eager to play him off against his former employer, the ACS published his glowing accounts of life in the colony. Devany neglected to mention that within months of their arrival his wife and two children had died of malaria.

The pressure on James Forten to follow the lead of his former apprentice never let up. ACS officers called on him at his home and his place of business. He would listen politely to their arguments—he was renowned for being courteous to visitors, even if he disagreed with them—and then he would respond with arguments of his own. He understood that not every white person who advocated colonization was a defender of slavery. Some truly thought they were helping the enslaved and improving the situation of free people of color. How sad that such earnest souls had been deceived by the ACS.

If James Forten would not back the ACS, an old ally would…at least for a while. As senior bishop of the rapidly growing African Methodist Episcopal denomination, Richard Allen may have hoped to set up mission stations in Liberia with the help of the ACS. Whether or not that was the case, in 1827 Allen tipped off ACS officer William B. Davidson about a new development. A man named Samuel Cornish had arrived in Philadelphia, and he was planning to establish an anti-ACS newspaper with help from none other than James Forten. Davidson was aghast. "The ideas of Cornish & Forten are that the people of Colour…are by birth entitled to all the rights of freemen" in the United States, not on a distant African shore.

Cornish and Forten were old friends. Samuel Cornish's brother worked in the Forten sail-loft, and he himself had spent some years as a preacher in Philadelphia before relocating to New York City. In 1827 he represented a group of black New Yorkers who believed the time had come for people of color to have a press to defend their interests. Their new paper was called *Freedom's Journal*. At the founding meeting Cornish was appointed senior editor. John B. Russwurm, one of the first black men in the United States to receive a college degree, became junior editor. Fund-raising got under way in various communities, including Philadelphia. James Forten was pleased to contribute, knowing *Freedom's Journal* would give him a powerful weapon in his crusade against the colonization society. Once the newspaper was up and running, Forten did indeed use it to gain publicity for his views on colonization. No wonder Mr. Davidson was worried.

Despite James Forten's very public opposition, the ACS leadership continued its efforts to win him over. Had he chosen, he could almost certainly have ended his days as the first president of Liberia. The influence he enjoyed in Philadelphia, home to one of the largest and most sophisticated free black communities in the nation, coupled with his success in business, made him a man the ACS desperately wanted to recruit, but he would have nothing to do with an organization he had come to loathe and fear.

Still, the ACS made one important convert. When Cornish stepped down from the editorship of *Freedom's Journal*, Russwurm took it over, but he became dejected. Although it got off to a good start, *Freedom's Journal* was soon on the verge of bankruptcy. Promises by the ACS to appoint him editor of the *Liberia Herald* worked a transformation upon Russwurm. James Forten, Samuel Cornish, and many other Northern free people were appalled when he suddenly announced that he planned to go to Liberia.

There were other reasons for James Forten to worry. In 1829 the Pennsylvania legislature endorsed the ACS. Even old friends were jumping on the bandwagon. Richard Peters Jr., Forten's lawyer and a member of the Pennsylvania Abolition Society, had become convinced that the ACS could advance the abolitionist agenda. In James Forten's mind, that was why the organization was so dangerous. It appealed not only to the avowed enemies of black Americans but also to many of their staunchest friends. It was fooling them as it had once fooled him. Still, he refused to abandon the struggle. Bleak though the situation seemed by the end of the 1820s, the next decade would bring him powerful new allies in his battle against the American Colonization Society—as well as a new crop of enemies.

CHAPTER FOURTEEN

Allies in Liberty's Cause

As the 1820s drew to a close, there was no let-up in James Forten's war against the American Colonization Society. Everywhere he looked he seemed to see the forces of the ACS at work, trying to "persuade" free people of color to emigrate with extravagant promises of a better life in Liberia. The society was also directing a great deal of propaganda at well-intentioned whites. It was making converts and bringing in donations from men and women who sincerely opposed slavery. That was why Forten saw it as so dangerous. The white antislavery movement was going in what he regarded as entirely the wrong direction—accepting vague promises about how and when the ACS would do away with slavery, and at the same time coming around to the point of view that people like himself—black people born in America—somehow "belonged" in Africa.

James Forten had never refused to work with white people who shared his commitment to the elimination of slavery and its twin evil, prejudice, but by 1830 he believed many of his old friends had grown lukewarm. Although the Pennsylvania Abolition Society struggled on valiantly, it had experienced a wave of defections.

Awakened to the volatile nature of the slavery issue at the national level, dozens of members had resigned or simply become inactive, comforting themselves with the hope that slavery would die out in a generation or two. Just as bad in Forten's mind was trusting the promises of the ACS that it could solve all of America's racial problems. He still had his circle of white antislavery friends, most of them Quakers. Thomas Shipley and Joseph Parrish, Isaac T. Hopper, and the tireless antislavery newspaper editor Benjamin Lundy all enjoyed his affection and trust. James and Lucretia Mott were frequent visitors to the Forten home. Through them the family came to know Sarah and Angelina Grimké, the sisters who had chosen exile from their native South Carolina and separation from their rich and influential family rather than continue to lead lives of privilege based on the exploitation of slave labor. Still, in 1830 organized antislavery seemed weak when compared to the power and wealth ranged against it. If James Forten was depressed from time to time, he had reason to be; but he was about to find an ally who would inject new life into the movement.

At first glance, James Forten had nothing in common with William Lloyd Garrison, a white New Englander half his age. Despite the differences in their backgrounds, though, the two men were drawn together as friends and co-workers. What created a bond between them was a passionate commitment to ending slavery. William Lloyd Garrison was a less than successful newspaper editor when he and James Forten first became acquainted. Like Forten, Garrison had known dire poverty in his early years, and like Forten he had struggled to learn a skilled trade. He had served an apprenticeship to a printer in his hometown of Newburyport, Massachusetts, and then become a printer himself, editing a succession of short-lived papers.

His growing sense that slavery was a sin that must be eradicated led Garrison into a partnership with Forten's friend Benjamin

Lundy. Like Lundy, Garrison initially regarded colonization as a necessary evil that might ease the sufferings of at least some of those in bondage in the South. However, as his friendship with James Forten and others in the Northern free black community grew, he rejected the ACS's agenda and became outspoken in his opposition to it.

William Lloyd Garrison (1835)
Society Portrait Collection, Historical Society of Pennsylvania
This portrait was painted by a young African American artist,
Robert Douglass Jr., who was a friend of the Forten family.

In 1829 Garrison joined Benjamin Lundy in Baltimore as co-editor of the *Genius of Universal Emancipation,* a paper James Forten subscribed to and the entire Forten family read. Garrison ran into trouble when he used the *Genius* to criticize a New England ship-owner who was involved in shipping slaves from one state to another. Convicted by a court in Maryland of malicious libel, Garrison spent a month and a half in jail until white New York merchant Arthur Tappan, a fellow abolitionist, paid his fine. Garrison left jail determined to start his own antislavery newspaper, more militant in tone than the *Genius*. He would need backers, though, because he had no money.

James Forten was one of the first people Garrison contacted. Garrison's letter requesting support has not survived, but Forten's enthusiastic reply has. He was delighted to hear about the newspaper, which Garrison proposed to call the *Liberator*. Forten wrote that he had told all of his friends about it and had persuaded twenty-seven of them to take out subscriptions. He sent their names and addresses to Garrison. He also sent the young editor a banker's draft for $54 to cover the cost of the subscriptions until he could get the individual subscribers to pay up. Garrison was overjoyed. The first issue of the *Liberator* rolled off the printing press in Boston (the city Garrison decided to make his base of operations) on New Year's Day, 1831. In the second issue Garrison published an excerpt from James Forten's letter of support. He did not name Forten, but he observed: "We are acquainted with the writer, and very proud...of his friendship."

A few weeks later Garrison printed another letter "from the intelligent and highly respectable gentleman alluded to in our second number." James Forten praised the *Liberator's* firm stand against colonization. He pointed to the irony that a man like himself, who had fought for independence and whose family had lived in Pennsylvania since the 1680s, was constantly being told "that Africa is my country." If he had toyed with racial separation back in 1817, he now declared that to try to separate black Americans and white Americans "is as impossible as to bail out the Delaware with a bucket." They were one people.

Week after week, through the pages of the *Liberator*, James

Forten reached out to an audience of reformers, black and white. He asked Garrison to keep his identity a secret, and Garrison did so. Forten used as his pen-name "A Colored Philadelphian." He wrote about a whole series of related topics. If Garrison wanted a forceful condemnation of slavery, a brief essay on the evils of racial prejudice, or an indictment of the American Colonization Society, James Forten would supply it. In one of his letters, for instance, he described how prejudice kept black Americans trapped in the lowest paid jobs because so few white craftsmen would teach them a skilled trade. (He always acknowledged how fortunate he had been to have had Robert Bridges as a friend and patron.) He challenged "our pretended white friends" who were so keen to send him and every other free black person to Liberia to spend their time and money at home, educating people of color and "secur[ing] to them all the rights...of freemen." Then "it would soon be found...that they made as good citizens as the whites."

Masthead of the first issue of the *Liberator*
Library Company of Philadelphia
James Forten provided fifty-four dollars, a considerable sum of
money at the time, to help Garrison buy the supplies of paper
and ink he needed for the first issue of the *Liberator.*

In the *Liberator* of August 20, 1831 Garrison published an especially forceful piece by James Forten under the caption "Men Must Be Free." Forten had written it in reaction to a report about a rash of fires in Fayetteville, North Carolina. He believed the fires were "a visitation from God" for the sins of the slave-holders. He had heard from a friend from Fayetteville about the savage beating of a free black man in the neighborhood who had dared to joke about the fires. Was it not disgusting, Forten asked, that such a thing could happen "in this boasted land of liberty?" He added: "When we…hear of almost every nation fighting for its liberty, is it to be expected that the African race will continue always in the degraded state they are now? No. The time is fast approaching when the words 'Fight for liberty, or die in the attempt,' will be sounded in every African ear."

That time was approaching more rapidly than James Forten could have imagined. His letter was published on August 20, 1831. On the night of August 21, in Southampton County, Virginia, scores of slaves, led by the charismatic Nat Turner, rose up against their masters, with every intention of winning their liberty or dying in the attempt.

In the wake of the bloody rampage in Virginia James Forten sent an anxious letter to Garrison. He feared for his friend's safety. Southern whites were panting for vengeance, insisting that Turner and his men had been inspired to rebel after getting their hands on copies of the *Liberator* and similar publications. The attitude of the slave-owners shocked Forten to the core. He could not believe that "they should still close their eyes, and seek to find the cause from without, when all the materials are so plentiful within." Did they honestly think that their slaves were happy? Could they be so stupid as to imagine that Turner and his followers had needed to be stirred up by people in the North? And yet that appeared to be the case. Forten understood that some Southern lawmakers had placed a bounty on Garrison's head, determined to silence both the *Liberator* and its courageous editor. Although slaveholders had failed to heed the lessons of "the late tragedy," Forten still hoped something good would come out of so much suffering and that people would awaken to the true cause of the rebellion. "Indeed, we live in stirring times, and every day brings news of some fresh effort for liberty, either at home or abroad—onward, onward, is indeed the watchword."

William Lloyd Garrison was never a rich man. He lived simply and did his best to increase the *Liberator's* circulation, but financial disaster loomed often. The majority of his subscribers, black and white, were people of modest means. Subscriptions went unpaid or had to be canceled during tough economic times. People shared their copies of the paper with their friends. That was all well and good when it came to getting the word out about the evils of slavery, but it boded ill for the financial well-being of the *Liberator*. Whenever a crisis loomed, Garrison was forced to beg for help, and one of the people he could always count on to come to his aid was James Forten. Forten never turned down a plea from Garrison. He helped him with his short-term cash-flow problems and made substantial loans to him to keep the newspaper afloat. A far more experienced man of business than Garrison, and a great deal more organized, he also offered sound advice about the best ways to market the *Liberator*.

Over the years James Forten gave generously to various initiatives Garrison told him about, and in 1831 he believed there was another one that deserved his support. Garrison, the wealthy New Yorker Arthur Tappan who had gotten Garrison out of jail, and white evangelical preacher Simeon S. Jocelyn came up with a plan to establish a college for young black men. It would have a farm and workshops as well as traditional classrooms, and the idea was that students could learn practical skills while also getting a good classical education. They would learn Greek and blacksmithing, mathematics and shoe-making. What was produced on the farm and in the workshops would be sold, and that would keep costs low. It seemed an excellent idea, especially since the college was to be established in a place that was already a center of learning. It would be located in New Haven, Connecticut, practically next door to Yale University.

African American leaders in Philadelphia and other communities in the North thought this was a splendid plan. They looked forward to being able to send their sons to the college and they began raising funds to buy land and start building. It is easy to see why James Forten lent *his* name to the project. It had been developed by three white reformers he respected, and it offered young men precisely the kinds of opportunities he thought they should have. Without the chance to learn a skilled trade, people of color would continue to be at the bottom of the economic heap.

James Forten and the other supporters of the college were in for a nasty shock. When the authorities in New Haven learned of the plan to locate the college in their midst they immediately blocked it. Rev. Jocelyn, who had been born and raised in New Haven, fought valiantly for the college. He addressed a huge public meeting, putting forward every argument he could think of, from civic pride to economic self-interest, but no one would listen to him. James Forten was appalled when he read the published proceedings of the New Haven meeting. He could not believe that "in that large assemblage, but one friend was to be found to stand up in our behalf."

It was the same a year or two later. White Quaker teacher Prudence Crandall provoked the wrath of her community in Canterbury, Connecticut when she admitted the daughter of a local black farmer to her previously all-white school. The furious reaction of Canterbury's white residents prompted her to consider transforming her school into one exclusively for black students. Garrison encouraged her and gave her introductions to his friends, among them James Forten. Forten had no daughters available to send to her school. Harriet was married, Margaretta and Sarah were too old, and Mary's health was too poor for her parents to think of letting her leave home. However, he could at least lend Crandall his name and the weight it carried in the African American community.

Forten's enthusiastic endorsement might have persuaded other black parents to entrust their daughters to Prudence Crandall's care, but it could not save her school. Enraged white residents of Canterbury and the surrounding communities attacked the building, constantly harassed Crandall and her pupils, and finally jailed her for breaking a brand new law forbidding the education of out-of-state black people in Connecticut.

In the face of intense opposition to every measure they came up with to end slavery and improve the lives of black people in America, James Forten, William Lloyd Garrison, and the growing number of antislavery radicals pressed on. In 1833 Forten helped pay for Garrison's trip to Britain to raise funds and denounce the American Colonization Society. It had not escaped the attention of either Forten or Garrison that ACS agent Elliott Cresson was in Britain telling antislavery sympathizers there that the colony of Liberia was the salvation of people of color. Something must be done to stop him winning new allies across the Atlantic.

Both before and after Garrison's highly successful trip to Britain, James Forten and the members of his extended family aided him with everything at their disposal—money, hospitality, introductions to their friends, and their own deep affection. They also aided him with information. James Forten had an inexhaustible fund of information, all of it negative, on Liberia and the ACS. He observed to Garrison that, as one of Philadelphia's leading sailmakers, "I am well acquainted with all the Masters of Vessels belonging to this Port that have been to the Coast of Africa." They told him plenty about Liberia.

James Forten had other sources as well. In 1831 he summarized for Garrison the contents of a letter he had just received from an old friend in Liberia that told the tragic tale of the Mars family from Ohio. Thirty-one members had died since arriving in the colony. ACS supporters challenged Forten on his facts when the story appeared in the *Liberator*, but it was proven to be substantially true.

James Forten had an exceptionally good intelligence-gathering network in Liberia, and at the heart of it was none other than John B. Russwurm's business partner, Joseph R. Dailey. Dailey was someone the Forten family had known and trusted for years. Yes, he had chosen to go to Liberia, something James Forten felt no sensible free person of color should do, but he was making amends by exposing the true state of affairs in the colony. Although enthusiastic about Liberia to begin with, Dailey had soon changed his tune. His accounts of life in Liberia were devastating. Letter after letter hammered home the same message. People were dying in droves. The colony was bankrupt, and the ACS was doing nothing to help the settlers. Every letter James Forten received from Dailey he forwarded to Garrison, who printed excerpts in the *Liberator*. The ACS knew it had a traitor in the ranks, but many months went by before ACS officers identified Dailey, and by then the damage had been done. James Forten made sure of that.

Despite James Forten's best efforts, the ACS continued to find otherwise well-intentioned white people prepared to donate money to advance its agenda. On June 24, 1833 local supporters held a rally at Philadelphia's Musical Fund Hall. Men Forten respected, like ship-owner Thomas P. Cope and William White, the senior bishop of his own denomination, took very active roles. ACS secretary Ralph R. Gurley spoke, as did Robert S. Finley, the son of ACS founder Rev. Robert Finley, who insisted that the society's southern supporters were benevolent people who cared about the welfare of their slaves. James Forten was probably among the "colored gentlemen" who called on Gurley and Finley the morning after the rally to let them know exactly what Philadelphia's free people of color thought of their organization.

Soon afterwards, Forten and his allies had another chance to make their views known. They arranged a meeting at which members of the black community could question three returning emigrants. The three told of mistreatment of the native peoples of Liberia by settlers and ACS officials, along with all manner of immoral behavior. They also told of sickness and death among the colonists. All three had lost family members.

As Forten and Garrison knew, though, there was no shortage of literature on the merits of colonization. Eventually Garrison decided the opposition must strike back. He would put together a pamphlet that would show white people just how bad the ACS really was and what black people thought of it. To do so he needed detailed information about the society. He turned to James Forten, who searched his files and sent Garrison anything he thought might be of use—the ACS's annual reports, clippings from its newspaper, letters, pamphlets, speeches—mounds of material that Garrison found invaluable. When *Thoughts on African Colonization* appeared, James Forten was very pleased. The pamphlet exposed what he insisted was the duplicity of the ACS and also made it abundantly clear how most free people of color viewed colonization.

The ACS was deeply concerned, and it had reason to be. After reading in *Thoughts on African Colonization* how vehemently James Forten and others in the black community opposed the society, Arthur Tappan, who had given the ACS thousands of dollars in the sincere belief that it was working to end slavery, began to rethink his generosity. He visited Philadelphia, talked with Forten and other prominent African Americans, and soon cut his ties to the ACS. Forten was delighted. The pamphlet had achieved one major victory and he looked forward to more.

One of the documents Garrison reprinted in his pamphlet was the set of resolutions passed at the meeting at Mother Bethel back in January 1817. James Forten had chaired that meeting at a time when he himself was still wavering about African colonization, but by the time Garrison's pamphlet went to press Forten was insisting that he and his entire community had *always* known the scheme was a bad one. Was that dishonest? A little, perhaps, but then by the early 1830s he *knew* just how bad the ACS's agenda was. When abolitionists like Arthur Tappan, who had supported the ACS because they thought it was committed to freeing all the slaves in America, asked James Forten about the 1817 meeting, he gave them his version of it. He insisted that "even then, at the very onset, when the monster came in a guise to deceive some of our firmest friends," black people had seen the ACS for what it really was. He said not a word about his initial enthusiasm for the colonization scheme.

Despite his long years of cooperation with the Pennsylvania Abolition Society, James Forten had never been invited to become a member. The PAS was an all-white organization and remained so for decades. Forten worked with the men in the PAS and maintained close friendships with a number of them. However, when the chance came to join forces with Garrison and the white antislavery radicals, he embraced the opportunity.

Garrison and his allies in New England saw the need to give their brand of antislavery a strong foundation. They had to mobilize, and they proceeded to do so. Antislavery societies sprang up across New England and the Mid-Atlantic states, and by the fall of 1833 Garrison and others in the movement decided it was time to form a national society. Where should they rally? Boston? New York? No, the city they considered most fitting for *their* great undertaking was the same one where the Founding Fathers had gathered almost half a century before. They would meet in Philadelphia.

Invitations went out, and in early December sixty-two delegates convened at the Adelphi Building on Fifth and Walnut Streets in the heart of Philadelphia. Three of the delegates were men of color—James G. Barbadoes, one of Garrison's most zealous co-workers from Boston, Philadelphia barber and dentist James McCrummill, and Robert Purvis. James Forten could surely have had a place among this new group of "founding fathers" if he had wanted it, but he stepped back in favor of his young friend. Forten was in his late sixties. It was time for the younger generation to move to the forefront. Although he was not among the delegates, James Forten was almost certainly among the scores of onlookers at the Adelphi. And during the course of the convention many of the delegates took the time to visit him and his family.

James Forten approved on the American Anti-Slavery Society's Declaration of Sentiments, especially since it explicitly linked the abolitionists to the "band of patriots" who had sought freedom from British tyranny in 1776. Like them, the abolitionists would go to war to achieve their goals, but they pledged to fight only with "the power of love." They rejected any idea of gradual emancipation. Every slave must be set free at once. They also condemned any colonization scheme, even if its defenders claimed it would bring about the end of slavery. As he listened to the proceedings, James Forten could feel very pleased indeed. His message had come through loud and clear.

Year after year James Forten, his two eldest sons, James Jr. and Robert, and their ally Robert Purvis were elected to office in the American Anti-Slavery Society. Increasing age and the need to oversee his business kept Forten himself close to home, and he chose not to travel to New York City, where the annual meetings were generally held, but the three younger men were often present as delegates. At the local level he helped establish the Philadelphia Anti-Slavery Society, while James Forten Jr., Robert B. Forten, Robert Purvis, and a number of their friends joined several dozen white abolitionists to found the Young Men's Anti-Slavery Society of Philadelphia. Young and old alike saw the need for a radical anti-slavery organization at the state level. The result was the formation

in 1837 of the Pennsylvania Anti-Slavery Society, which was affili-
ated with the American Anti-Slavery Society. At age seventy James
Forten thought this was so important that he made the trek to
Harrisburg to be present at the inaugural meeting.

The men who organized the American Anti-Slavery Society
aimed at racial inclusiveness—black and white were welcome to
join—but not women. Garrison and the other men told women
abolitionists to form their own societies, and they did. In December 1833, within days of the birth of the American Anti-Slavery
Society, Charlotte Forten, three of her daughters, and a future
daughter-in-law helped found the Philadelphia Female Anti-Slavery Society.

During the 1830s and into the 1840s abolition was at the core
of the Forten family's social life. They attended antislavery meetings. They helped fund the *Liberator* and the other abolitionist jour-
nals that began to appear as the movement gained strength. They
raised money for the antislavery cause and they found various ways
to help the scores of runaway slaves from the South who sought
refuge in Philadelphia. They also hosted their fellow abolitionists.
Garrison visited regularly and was universally beloved. In their letters to friends in Philadelphia, Sarah and Angelina Grimké often
asked to be remembered to the Fortens. Others involved in the
movement begged to be introduced. George Thompson, a British
abolitionist who had met Robert Purvis in London, wrote to let
Purvis know he would be visiting Philadelphia and wanted to meet
James Forten, about whom he had heard so much. Garrison's
brother-in-law, Henry Benson, recalled a most enjoyable evening
he had spent with Thompson and Garrison at the Forten home. It
was during another lively evening at 92 Lombard Street that Thompson met Angelina Grimké. By the mid-1830s James Forten and
his family had become antislavery celebrities and their home a hub
of abolitionist activity.

CHAPTER FIFTEEN

A Family Commitment

James Forten's children came of age as radical abolitionism was growing in strength. They forged friendships with white anti-slavery co-workers. They also made contact with others like themselves—wealthy and well-educated young black people committed to a controversial cause. Their very presence served that cause, helping white antislavery advocates disprove notions that black people were somehow intellectually inferior to whites. Of course, being on display, "a credit to the race," was not always a comfortable feeling, but they accepted it as gracefully as they could, and James Forten had the pleasure of seeing his children and his much-loved son-in-law emerge as articulate champions of the cause he had struggled to advance for so many years.

On September 3, 1831, Robert Purvis, whom James Forten already looked upon as a son, truly became a member of the family when he married Harriet Forten. The wedding was a private one at the Forten home. There was a last-minute crisis when a death in the family of the white minister serving St. Thomas's prevented him from performing the ceremony. However, it was a sign of James Forten's standing that the assistant bishop of the diocese stepped in to take his place.

Robert Purvis had all the qualities James and Charlotte Forten could wish for in a son-in-law, and he was rich as well. For the first few months of their married life Robert and Harriet lived at 92 Lombard Street with her parents, and then Robert bought a home nearby. Towards the end of 1832 Harriet and Robert presented James and Charlotte with their first grandchild, William.

Robert and Harriet became increasingly involved in the work of antislavery, she through her membership of the Philadelphia Female Anti-Slavery Society and he through a number of organizations. They wrote, raised funds, and routinely defied the law by sheltering runaway slaves in their home.

In 1834 Robert made a trip to Britain to meet abolitionists in England and Scotland and to settle his father's estate. There was some talk of Harriet going with him, but she had William to care for, and she was pregnant again. Robert went alone, sailing from New York. He had planned to leave from Philadelphia, but a prominent white Southerner, Bernard Carter, had heard that a black man had booked passage on the same ship as himself, and he objected very strongly. The ship-owners begged Robert to sail on another ship.

Robert's trip was a great success. He had letters of introduction to prominent British abolitionists, and they made him welcome. They took him to tourist sites, including the Houses of Parliament. On Robert's visit to the House of Commons his host spotted the champion of Irish rights, Daniel O'Connell, and attempted to introduce Robert to him. Assuming that the light-skinned Robert was a white Southerner, O'Connell stalked off. After a few hurried words of explanation, however, he turned around and greeted Robert most warmly. He told Robert that he loathed slavery and would never knowingly have anything to do with anyone who supported it. Robert was delighted. He never forgot Daniel O'Connell's words, and from that point on he himself became a friend of Irish independence.

By an odd coincidence, on his way back to the United States Robert found himself booked to sail on the same ship as Bernard Carter. Carter failed to recognize Robert Purvis as a man of color and struck up a friendship with him. Other passengers followed suit, and Robert became a great favorite. On the last night of the voyage he arranged a little surprise. To the amusement of everyone except Carter, he revealed his true identity.

During the months Robert was touring England and Scotland, Harriet was attending meetings of the Female Anti-Slavery Society with her mother and sisters. Her antislavery work became an extension of her husband's, and she happily accepted that. He traveled, but she stayed closer to home, running the household and raising their children. She was happy for it to be that way. She and Robert had an ideal partnership. Her younger sister, Sarah, on the other hand, had a rather different outlook on life, and a different view of marriage.

Sarah Forten was a feisty young woman, opinionated, sometimes outspoken, and not exactly eager to accept a secondary role to a husband. She emerged as a talented antislavery poet. She had apparently already been trying her hand at writing when the *Liberator* began publishing and Garrison put out a general request for poetry and prose pieces to help fill the columns of his newspaper. Sarah sent him a poem she titled "The Grave of the Slave." It was January 1831, she was just sixteen years old, and within a week or two of sending her poem off to Garrison she had the thrill of seeing it in print. It was eventually set to music and sung at antislavery rallies.

Sarah wanted her work judged on its own merits. She didn't want Garrison to publish it because her father was one of his most generous supporters. For that reason she used a pen-name, "Ada." She followed up her first effort with more poems, and Garrison thought well enough of them to publish them all and beg the unknown writer to send more. "Ada's" identity remained a secret until her father uncovered it and told Garrison. Undeterred, Sarah kept writing—about the miseries the slaves endured, about the splitting up of black families on the auction block, and above all about the nation's betrayal of its founding principles of freedom and justice for all. She was very much her father's daughter.

Her contact with abolitionists and reformers energized Sarah and broadened her horizons. She developed a friendship with Elizabeth Whittier, sister of the poet John Greenleaf Whittier, and through Elizabeth she met and corresponded with other white female abolitionists. Sarah greatly admired the Grimké sisters, and she felt comfortable enough to respond to a letter from Angelina Grimké asking about the impact of prejudice upon herself and her family. Sarah acknowledged how frustrated she was at seeing "many…preferred before me, who by education, birth, or worldly circumstances were no better than myself, THEIR sole claim to notice depending on the superior advantage of being *White*." Sarah's honest and very direct answer to the white abolitionist's query obviously helped Angelina Grimké understand the impact of prejudice at the personal level.

Sarah postponed marriage until 1838, when she was 23. She wed a man she had known for years—her brother-in-law, Joseph Purvis. Joseph was sympathetic to abolitionism, but he was not the antislavery activist that his brother Robert was. He was a country gentleman. Sarah moved with him to the farm he had bought. It was too far from Philadelphia for her to attend antislavery meetings on a regular basis. Sadder still, she stopped writing, too preoccupied with raising children (she and Joseph had eight in twelve years) and running a farm to have a spare moment for anything else.

James and Charlotte Forten's eldest child, Margaretta, never married. She became a teacher, and she also devoted a great amount of time to the Philadelphia Female Anti-Slavery Society. Like Sarah, she wrote antislavery poetry. If not of the same quality as her sister's, it obviously struck a chord with her fellow abolitionists, and some of it found its way into print.

Vase of Flowers
Amy Matilda Cassey Album, Library Company of Philadelphia
This painting and a short poem that appeared with it were the
handiwork of James Forten's eldest daughter, Margaretta.

The youngest of the Forten daughters, Mary Isabella, was an invalid and essentially home-bound, but she read extensively and she, too, wrote poetry. Unfortunately, her poor health kept her from involving herself in antislavery work as energetically as the other members of her family.

As for the Forten sons, by the early 1830s James Jr. and Robert Bridges Forten were proving that they had made good use of the education their parents had given them. They were articulate, well-read, and obviously dedicated to abolition. James Forten took great pride in them and was pleased to have their talents recognized.

For Garrison's information, James Forten wrote him in March 1831 to identity "F," whose letter Garrison had just published in the *Liberator*, as 18-year-old James Jr. In his letter "F" had described his pleasure in reading the *Liberator*. "Its columns most unquestionably convince us that the spirit of liberty is awakened." He feared for the future of a country that rejoiced in "the downfall of tyranny in foreign nations," while permitting slavery to continue within its own borders. "The time cannot be far distant, when Justice, armed more powerful[ly] than human aid can afford, will break the bonds of oppression, and wield the scepter of liberty and independence throughout the nation." Like his sister Sarah, and the rest of his siblings, James Forten Jr. had obviously been influenced by his father's teachings.

By the time he was in his early twenties, James Forten Jr. was much in demand as an antislavery speaker. He spoke to groups such as the Philadelphia Female Anti-Slavery Society, drawing attention not to slavery alone but to the evils of prejudice in all its forms. He recognized that his father's wealth had given him advantages few other young black men enjoyed, and he felt it was his duty to use his privileged position to help others less fortunate than himself. He became a charter member of the Library Company of Colored Persons, an organization he and his friends hoped would "add something to the general char[ac]ter of our people for the improvement of our intellectual faculties." He spoke and sang (he reportedly had a fine singing voice) at antislavery rallies and, like his siblings, he wrote antislavery poetry.

James and Charlotte were pleased with their eldest son's choice of a wife. Jane Vogelsang was a member of a socially prominent black family in New York City. Her father, Peter, had come to the United States from the West Indies. He was a fervent abolitionist and also a successful businessman. He had been able to give Jane the same kind of education the Fortens had given their daughters. The wedding of James Forten Jr. and Jane Vogelsang took place in New York City on January 13, 1839, and the couple came to live at 92 Lombard Street with James's parents.

Title Page of the Martina Dickerson Album
Library Company of Philadelphia
James Forten Jr. produced this ornate title page for
his friend Martina Dickerson's album.

Like his older brother, Robert Bridges Forten was an eloquent
public speaker. He spoke out on slavery, on the evils of alcohol,
and on the benefits of education—for women as well as men. He
was an accomplished mathematician and an enthusiastic amateur
astronomer. He even made his own telescope, which was put on
exhibition at the renowned Franklin Institute. A romantic young
man, Robert soon formed a deep attachment to one of his sisters'
friends, Mary Virginia Wood.

The Fortens knew Mary and her sister, Annie, almost as well as
they knew the Purvises. Mary and Annie Wood had arrived in Phila-

delphia in the early 1830s from Hertford, a small town in coastal North Carolina, and they apparently came alone. All the evidence—the money spent on their education, their removal from the South, their light complexions—points to one scenario: they were the biracial daughters of a well-to-do white man in the Hertford area. Mary and Annie's story resembled that of Robert and Joseph Purvis, except that William Purvis acknowledged his relationship with Harriet Judah and was honest and straightforward about the couple's children. The mysterious Mr. Wood, although he provided well for his daughters, preferred to keep their existence a secret from his white family.

Once she settled down in Philadelphia, Mary Wood became acquainted with the Forten family. Like most genteel young ladies, she had as one of her prized possessions an ornate leather-bound album. Almost all of the Fortens contributed a poem or two to her album, but the one who wrote most often was Robert. The friendship between the two blossomed into romance, and eventually Robert plucked up the courage to ask Mary to marry him. She accepted. Robert and Mary were married at St. Thomas's Church on October 18, 1836. Their first child, Charlotte, was born on August 17, 1837, in her grandparents' home. The following year Robert and Mary left 92 Lombard Street for a home of their own. Their second child was born on May 15, 1839. They named him Gerrit Smith Forten in honor of a wealthy white abolitionist from upstate New York who was a frequent visitor to the Forten home and one of their dearest friends.

Thomas Willing Francis Forten, James and Charlotte Forten's third son, seems to have been rather limited intellectually and may have suffered from a mental impairment. Not so their youngest, William Deas Forten. In time he would make his mark as an abolitionist and a crusader for civil rights, but in the 1830s, while his older siblings were distinguishing themselves in the antislavery cause, he was only in his early teens. Even so, his parents had plans for him. In 1835, when William left the Pennsylvania Abolition Society's Clarkson School, they sent him to Oneida Institute in Whitesboro, New York, a school that accepted students without regard to race. Oneida was run on the manual labor system, just like the college that had been planned for New Haven.

William was 12 or 13 when he was packed off to Oneida, so he began his studies in the "juvenile" department. He did not stay long enough to graduate to the "senior" program. Perhaps he was home-sick. Perhaps he was not sufficiently well prepared for the rigorous course of study. Regardless, his father's enthusiasm for the school endured long after William left. James Forten continued to help support it financially, and he and Robert Purvis helped pay for scholarships for poor but deserving black students.

The Forten children inherited a great deal from their father, but their mother also had a major influence on their lives. When Charlotte Vandine Forten features in visitors' descriptions of the household at 92 Lombard Street, it is as James Forten's faithful and con-scientious wife, and as the mother of a group of talented young men and women, but seldom as a force in her own right. Bearing nine children and raising eight of them, overseeing a large house-hold, and entertaining all and sundry left little time for anything else. However, Charlotte did have interests beyond her immediate family circle. She was a zealous member of her church. She was active in the Philadelphia Female Anti-Slavery Society. She had her own friends, some black and some white. And occasionally she found an odd moment to write a poem for a young friend's album.

In the 1830s the Forten home was alive with antislavery activ-ity. Few abolitionists who visited the city missed the chance to call at 92 Lombard. What they saw and heard fascinated them. James Forten cut an imposing figure. At six feet in height, he literally tow-ered over most of his guests. Witty and well-informed on a whole range of topics, he was well worth listening to, and the story of his remarkable life enthralled visitor after visitor. Charlotte, gracious and kind, made her home a place where guests always felt welcome. But James and Charlotte were increasingly willing to step back and let their children be the focus of attention. They had given them the finest education they could. How their children used that education, and how they showed in their individual lives the lessons their parents had taught them about the duties that came with the privileges they enjoyed, would help shape the course of organized antislavery and social reform in Philadelphia and beyond. Freeborn, well-educated and wealthy they might be, but their parents had never intended that they should turn their backs on the less fortunate members of the black community. Their feelings might be bruised by the occasional insensitive remark from their white abolitionist allies. They might feel uncomfortable at being put on display. But they knew and understood that the millions in slavery in the South endured far more than wounded feelings. The abolitionist cause was their cause, just as it was their parents' cause. James and Charlotte Forten had raised their children well, and their pride in them was fully justified.

CHAPTER SIXTEEN

Law-Breakers and Lawmakers

W hat white abolitionists did not always understand was that freedom from slavery was not the same as full citizenship. Every day of their lives, free people of color grappled with the reality of discrimination. Their presence was tolerated, nothing more. And the racial violence that broke out in so many communities in the 1830s made it painfully clear that their presence might not continue to be tolerated. James Forten was no stranger to the depths of racism. Despite his optimism about the liberalizing "spirit of the times," he knew there would be more battles before the day of jubilee. As he soon discovered, though, the battles of the 1830s would be fiercer and bloodier than any he had experienced up to that point.

On November 23, 1831, a bunch of young white men met at a tavern near James Forten's sail-loft to discuss a matter of the utmost urgency. They were sure Nat Turner and his rebels had been incited to violence by free people of color and their fanatical white friends. What the young men were *really* upset about, though, was not so much the death and destruction in Virginia but the impact closer to home. They feared that hordes of free black people would

flee the South as enraged Southern whites sought vengeance for
the lives that Turner and his men had taken. Where would the black
refugees go? The young men predicted they would come surging
into Pennsylvania, and they demanded action from the state legislature to keep them out.

Politicians took note. By the end of the year a bill was being
debated, and its provisions were enough to strike fear into everyone in the African American community. Black people from out of
state must pay five hundred dollars apiece for the right to live in
Pennsylvania. A family of six, for example—a mother, father, and
four children—would have to come up with three thousand dollars. Every black person, even those born in Pennsylvania, must
register with the authorities. Employers who knowingly hired un-
registered black workers could be fined. And the state would crack
down on runaway slaves who crossed into Pennsylvania from the
South.

A similar bill in 1813 had prompted James Forten to write *Letters from a Man of Colour*. Now, almost two decades later, he knew
he could not ignore this new threat. He had to do something, and
do it quickly. He rallied Robert Purvis and William Whipper, a recent arrival from Columbia, Pennsylvania who was making a name
for himself in Philadelphia as a community organizer, and they
launched a public relations initiative. They drew up a petition and
got a sympathetic lawmaker to present it to his colleagues in Harrisburg. In that petition they took on the proposed law point by
point. They spoke of their pride in Pennsylvania's tradition of freedom. Surely its citizens were too fair-minded to back this dreadful
new law. As for the state's black population, weren't its members,
by and large, decent, law-abiding, hard-working people? Forten and
his allies insisted that was the case, and they presented facts and
figures to prove it.

House Bill 446 was eventually lost in committee, but black Philadelphians, James Forten among them, were soon forced to confront an unwelcome truth, namely that many whites simply did not want them around. The legislature was flooded with petitions demanding curbs on black immigration into the state and urging support for the American Colonization Society in the hope of encouraging black people to depart for Liberia.

While some whites pursued legal means to restrict the black population, others were happy to use violence. On Independence Day in 1832 a vessel was docked in Philadelphia with almost a hundred African Americans on board. They were the newly freed slaves of a group of North Carolina Quakers, and they were on their way to Liberia, but a rumor started that they had come to stay in Philadelphia. A mob gathered and the captain was obliged to set sail immediately, without the much-needed supplies he had wanted to pick up before he and his passengers set out across the Atlantic.

A few weeks later there was a clash in one of Philadelphia's poorer neighborhoods. Although African Americans were actually on the receiving end of the violence, all of those arrested were black. Not a single white person was taken into custody. Similar confrontations occurred over the next eighteen months, but the first major explosion of violence came in the summer of 1834, and it involved James Forten's family.

All the ingredients for trouble were there. New York City had already experienced race riots, and Philadelphians were aware of that. They were also sweltering in an unusually hot and humid summer. Tempers were rising with the heat. One August evening James Forten sent his teenage son Thomas on an errand. The unfortunate lad was on his way home when a mob of young whites set upon him. He escaped without serious injury, and arrests were made, but it was merely a question of when, not if, there would be more trouble. It came just a few nights later in a stand-off between black and white youths at a carousel on South Street. A crowd of whites wrecked the carousel and then turned their attention to nearby black homes, barging in, destroying property, and beating anyone who did not flee. There were further outbreaks over the next couple of nights, and the authorities seemed powerless to do anything. Wisely the mobs stayed out of the neighborhood where James Forten and other prosperous black people lived. That neighborhood was also home to wealthy and well-connected whites, and they would demand a more effective police response. The rioting was concentrated in the poorer areas. Of course, there were white people in some of those areas, but they knew what was coming. They put candles in their windows and the rioters passed them by.

Although his immediate neighborhood was spared, James Forten received death threats, which he promptly reported to the mayor and the sheriff, both of whom offered to protect him. What was he guilty of, other than being black? In the minds of at least some whites in the city, it was his fault that black people refused to leave en masse for Liberia.

There was more trouble the next year. This time the mayor stopped the violence just as it was beginning, but he could not do anything about the unrest in Southwark, where James Forten had lived as a young man. Southwark was not technically part of the city and so it was outside the mayor's jurisdiction. The rioters concentrated their efforts there, looting homes and burning them to the ground. They spared women, children, and the elderly, but if they spotted any young black men in the course of their rampage they chased them down and beat them unmercifully. Individually or in small groups, some black residents tried to fight back, and several of them almost lost their lives in the attempt.

The Fortens could not insulate themselves from the waves of lawlessness sweeping across Philadelphia and its outlying districts like Southwark. In addition to the assault on James Forten's son and the threats against Forten himself in 1834, some of Forten's rental properties sustained damage in 1835. Two years later, on a peaceful Sunday afternoon in the summer of 1837, there was another riot in the making just yards from his front door. Quick action by the mayor prevented further unrest, but it was only a matter of time before the mob struck again.

Year after year the violence continued, often sparked by nothing more than an exchange of words, a look, a rumor. Generally the white perpetrators escaped punishment. As demoralizing as the continued outbreaks of rioting were, black Philadelphians, and in fact black people across the entire state of Pennsylvania, were about to suffer another assault, and this one would come not from so-called "midnight brawlers" but from the very men charged with making the law.

Could James Forten, or indeed any black man, vote in Pennsylvania? That question had no easy answer. The 1790 state constitution gave the right to vote to every "freeman" over 21 who paid a certain amount of property tax. By "freeman" had the framers meant any man who was free, or had they intended "freeman" to have a more complex meaning that applied only to whites? By the time anyone thought to ask that question, most of the men who had written the constitution were dead. Confusion reigned. Apparently, at some times and in some places in Pennsylvania, black men voted. At other times and in other places they either stayed home on election-day or were turned away from the polls. Philadelphia County was one of the areas where black men did not vote—and for good reason. A visitor from England recalled innocently asking a white acquaintance why black people did not come to the polls as their white neighbors did. The white Philadelphian snapped back, "Just let them try!"

Wisely, perhaps, James Forten and other well-to-do men of color in and around Philadelphia were reluctant to take up the question of voting rights. They feared what might happen, and anyway they had more pressing matters to attend to. And in a roundabout way James Forten *did* have a voice on election-day. In 1822 he explained to merchant Samuel Breck how he had helped him in his recent successful run for Congress. Forten told Breck that on election-day he had marched to the polls all fifteen of the white men in his sail-loft who were qualified to vote, and told them whom to vote for. The secret ballot was decades away, so Forten could indeed do what he said he had—take the men to the polling-place, remind them that he paid their wages, tell them that Mr. Breck was his friend, and then stand around to watch. Why should he push to have his right to vote upheld when he could command fifteen votes?

During the 1830s, though, the issue of voting rights surfaced repeatedly—not at first in Philadelphia but in rural counties, where property-owning black men were accustomed to vote and where for years their votes had been accepted without question. As white views hardened, more and more of these black "freemen" were turned away. They were understandably angry, and in some instances they sued, bringing the whole matter into the open.

Things became even more complicated in 1837. White Pennsylvanians decided to revise their state's constitution to bring it in line with the constitutions of most other states by doing away with the property qualification for voting. It did not seem right that men who were citizens in every other way should be unable to vote just because they did not own a certain amount of property. That was the way it had been in an earlier generation, but things were surely more democratic now.

The so-called Reform Convention met for its first session in Harrisburg, and several of the delegates spoke up on the matter of the black vote. It was time to be clear about what exactly a "freeman" was and add the word "white" to the new constitution. If not, once the property requirement was done away with, tens of thousands of black men—not just the select few who owned enough property to pay taxes—would turn up to vote. It would not make much difference in rural areas, where there were few black people anyway; but it could have a major impact in Philadelphia, where the black voting bloc could determine the outcome of an election. And what if a black man were to be elected to office? Did white Pennsylvanians want a man of color representing them in Congress? It was unthinkable, and they needed to act quickly to see that that never happened.

When they read in the newspapers what was being discussed in Harrisburg, the African American community, James Forten included, began to worry. Why couldn't white people just leave them alone? Did it hurt anyone to let "freeman" remain a vague and undefined term?

James Forten may have been present at a meeting in the summer of 1837 at which black Philadelphians drew up a petition to the Reform Convention. They explained that black people were good, honest citizens who valued their rights. The delegates were unimpressed, and one of them even brought up James Forten's name in their debates. Mr. Forten was a "black gentleman" who enjoyed "a respectable standing," but not even he could be allowed to vote. Let one black man vote, and hordes of ignorant ex-slaves would descend on Pennsylvania, eager to take up residence so they could cast their ballots on election-day.

During the summer and fall recess a number of things happened. First, reports of the debates awakened whites across the state to the fact that black men *were* voting in some counties. Then, in Bucks County, just outside Philadelphia, several dozen men of color did vote, as they had been accustomed to do for years. The unsuccessful candidate lost by a razor-thin margin. He sued, claiming that the votes of black men should not have been accepted because they were not and never had been "freemen." White people from communities all over Pennsylvania began bombarding the Reform Convention with petitions demanding action.

When the delegates reassembled after the recess, they gathered not in Harrisburg but in Philadelphia, not far from James Forten's home. Tensions mounted, and the Fortens and their friends followed every phase of the debate. More and more delegates were coming around to the point of view that black men must be prevented from imagining that they could vote. The word "white" must be added to the new constitution. The black community had its defenders. A handful of delegates declared that the idea that black men were not citizens was unfair and fundamentally un-American, but they were shouted down.

On the day the final vote was to be taken, the order was given to clear all black spectators from the gallery. Among those hustled out was James Forten Jr. Although he and his friends protested, it did no good. Most of the delegates had made up their minds. Again a courageous few spoke up on behalf of the state's black residents, but their colleagues ignored them and drafted a constitution that categorically denied men of color the right to vote. And yet again James Forten's name surfaced. One of the delegates sneered at "the yellow man—Fortune—who, by-the-by, had the *mis*-fortune to possess the wrong color," but who had "large real estate and…money in abundance." It did not matter that he had fought in the Revolution for liberty for all, or that he had lived an exemplary life, or that he was rich. What did matter was that he was not white.

The delegates finished their work and headed home. It was now up to the voters—the white voters—to accept or reject the new constitution. Robert Purvis, Robert B. Forten, and five other men of color authored a pamphlet they titled *The Appeal of Forty Thousand.* By their reckoning, that was the number of black men in Pennsylvania who were qualified to vote and would lose that right. The authors of the *Appeal* begged their fellow citizens to treat black people as *they* would wish to be treated. Surely men of color had earned the right to voice their opinions on election-day. And while they did not mention James Forten by name, they talked about black men who had endured "the horrors of the Jersey Prison Ship." Was it right, was it *American*, they asked, to deny the privileges of citizenship to those who had done so much to deserve them?

James Forten and his family helped raise funds to get the *Appeal* printed. Copies were sent to communities throughout Pennsylvania, but it did no good. Voters approved the new constitution by an overwhelming majority. A British Quaker, Joseph John Gurney, was in Philadelphia at the time and was shocked at what he heard. It was, he feared, a sign of worse to come. "I was told, that a white boy was observed seizing the marbles of a coloured boy in one of the streets, with the words, *'you have no rights now.'*" According to another account, the Fortens, the Purvises, and others hung black crape from their doors, just as they would have done if a family member had died. They were not mourning a relative, though. They were grieving over "departed liberty." They had good reason to mourn for "departed liberty." A new wave of violence was about to engulf the City of Brotherly Love.

CHAPTER SEVENTEEN

Keeping Hope Alive

P ennsylvania Hall was built by reformers, black and white, as a "temple of liberty," a place where they knew they could hold their meetings. Often, when they tried to rent a hall or a church to rally for an end to slavery or preach about the evils of alcohol, they were told the trustees would not hire out the place for anything controversial in case it came under attack by an angry mob. Tired of being turned away, the reformers made plans to build their own meeting-hall. Before long they had raised enough money to buy land and begin the construction of a handsome two-story building.

The opening of Pennsylvania Hall was scheduled for May 1838. The first major event was to be a female antislavery convention. Abolitionists and other reformers arrived from Boston and New York. Some were already acquainted with the Fortens. Others were friends of friends. A good many called at the Forten and Purvis homes. Harriet Purvis and her sisters planned to attend the women's convention. Her husband, her father, and two of her brothers were going to be at a meeting of the Pennsylvania Anti-Slavery Society in another part of the hall. Other events were planned. There were to be lectures on temperance and on the injustices being inflicted on the Cherokee and other Native peoples. Everyone was anticipating an intellectually stimulating few days.

Others in and around the city were looking with growing apprehension at what they saw as a social revolution in their midst—and they were not happy. White women belonged at home, not on the speaker's platform. Black women should be toiling as cooks and washerwomen in white households, not voicing their opinions on anything at all. Even more disturbing than women speaking in public were rumors of "race mixing." Someone spotted Harriet Purvis and the lighter-skinned Robert together and assumed they were an interracial couple. Someone else spied two "white" women with a "black" man and did not realize, first, that the three were cousins, and second, that they were all African American. Pennsylvania Hall was where all this scandalous behavior was being encouraged and where all this talk of rights for blacks, rights for women, rights for Indians was going on…Pennsylvania Hall must be destroyed.

"Destruction by Fire of Pennsylvania Hall"
Historical Society of Pennsylvania
This picture captures the fury of many white Philadelphians
over the issue of abolition.

On the first day of the women's antislavery convention a few dozen idlers gathered to shout insults. By the evening of the second day the size of the crowd had increased and the mood had grown uglier. As the delegates tried to listen to the speakers, a volley of stones crashed against the hastily shuttered windows. On the evening of the third day the mayor begged the women to leave because he feared for their safety. He took the keys, locked the place up, told the angry onlookers there would be no more meetings that evening, and went home.

The crowd waited until the mayor was out of sight before they broke in, trashed the place, turned on the gas jets, and watched the Hall burn to the ground. When firefighters arrived they left the Hall alone and simply wetted down neighboring buildings to stop them catching fire. They knew what the crowd wanted, and many of them felt the same way about the "temple of liberty." The destruction of Pennsylvania Hall was not the work of a bunch of lawless thugs. It was targeted and torched by "respectable" upper-middle-class white men who hated what the reformers stood for and feared for their business ties with Southern cotton planters if Philadelphia had the reputation of being a stronghold of antislavery sentiment.

In the face of so much anger James Forten refused to give up. He still hoped to change the hearts and minds of his white neighbors. An enlightened nation, he reasoned, would find injustice of any kind totally unacceptable. In the last years of his life he embarked on yet another crusade. His goal this time was nothing less than the transformation of American society. The American Moral Reform Society was the brainchild of James Forten, Robert Purvis, and William Whipper. Forten was the figurehead, but Whipper, who was half his age, was the driving force. It is only fair to say, though, that Forten and Whipper saw eye to eye on most things.

At the first meeting of the AMRS, held in Philadelphia in 1836, James Forten and his friends spoke out on the need for the entire nation to commit itself to the principles of "EDUCATION, TEMPER-ANCE, ECONOMY, AND UNIVERSAL LIBERTY." This was not an agenda for black Americans alone but for every man or woman who called America home. There were many in the black community in Phila-delphia and further afield who scoffed and said that Forten, Whip-per, Purvis and company were totally unrealistic. The reformers re-fused to back down. James Forten himself spoke to the AMRS con-vention about the changes he had seen in his long life. His home state had essentially abolished slavery, something that would have seemed unthinkable when he was a child. No, he wasn't saying free-dom from slavery was enough. He was not telling black people to accept second-class citizenship. Nor was he saying they should ig-nore the mobs who attacked their homes and assaulted them in the streets, or lawmakers who tried to take from them every right they had. He was fighting to make all people aware that the denial of lib-erty and equality must cease—and he had faith that in time that fundamental shift in attitudes would come about.

James Forten and his friends believed in educating people by giving them "the facts." Before the AMRS's 1837 convention they instructed delegates to collect statistics on the numbers of black people in their region of the country, their schools, their churches, their literary societies, the amount of land they owned, the jobs they held, and so forth. The idea was to prove to doubting whites that African Americans were hard-working and productive mem-bers of society who wanted the same things that they did—decent homes, decent jobs, education for themselves and their children. In short, black Americans and white Americans shared the same hopes and dreams. That was James Forten's message—the same one he had been preaching all of his adult life.

The AMRS's 1837 convention got under way in Philadelphia on the morning of August 14, and it was attended by delegates from communities across the North. James Forten gave the opening speech. However, although the carefully edited minutes tried to gloss over disagreements, the convention was far from harmonious. Trouble erupted when the committee appointed to draw up an agenda made its report. The first resolution read, "that we recommend to the free people of color the establishment of schools wherever it might be practical and safe." Whipper, Purvis, and several others protested against any phrase that singled out people according to race. That touched off a firestorm as some delegates declared that those who objected to the term "people of color" were ashamed of their African ancestry. The individuals they were criticizing snapped back that that was not the case. They were objecting only because they thought *all* Americans should be encouraged to establish schools. Back and forth the argument went, and it was difficult to get anything else done.

James Forten's old ally Samuel Cornish stirred things up even more. He was now the editor of the *Colored American,* the successor to *Freedom's Journal,* and he used it to criticize the American Moral Reform Society. He charged that it was "scattering its feeble efforts to the winds." James Forten was a "venerable" individual, but he could not keep the excitable delegates in check and he should resign as president.

What had gone so dreadfully wrong? Although Cornish and others jumped to the conclusion that Forten, Whipper, Purvis, and their faction were ashamed of being black, that was hardly the case. Their aim was to create a society in which race was simply irrelevant. They were striving for nothing less than a new understanding of what it meant to be an American. Unfortunately, they would soon discover that they were swimming against the tide. Outside of their own small group, black people did not want to hear them, and very few whites were willing to say that *they* saw race as unimportant.

Despite the growing chorus of criticism, James Forten and his friends pressed on. Another convention of the American Moral Reform Society met in Philadelphia in August 1838, and James Forten, just days short of his seventy-second birthday, mounted the speaker's platform to declare the meeting in session. It proved just as divisive as the previous one. The AMRS made no new converts and alienated some old ones. People were simply not ready for the radical message James Forten and the members of his circle were trying to spread.

As 1838 ended, James Forten reflected on a traumatic year. He and every other black "freeman" in Pennsylvania had lost the right to vote. Pennsylvania Hall was a burned-out shell, its ruins a stark reminder that few whites in his native city had any use for abolitionist "fanatics." As for his notion of creating an America in which race was not the measure of a person's worth, some of his oldest friends had told him he was a dreamer. Had his long career as a community leader come to an end? Was it time to retire? No. He would not back down. Foolish? Perhaps he was. Visionary? Certainly. But his battle to reform the nation was not one he was prepared to walk away from. He would see it through to the end.

CHAPTER EIGHTEEN

An Honest Man

As James Forten's life drew to a close, he and his community were spared the intense violence they had endured earlier in what had been a tumultuous decade. Did that mean white Philadelphians had become less hostile to the presence of black people in what they increasingly regarded as *their* city? No. In the four years following the burning of Pennsylvania Hall it just so happened that there was a brief let-up in the spate of riots Philadelphia suffered through. There would be plenty more to come. James Forten would not have to witness another mob rampaging through the city, but his wife and children would. Black people and black-owned buildings would continue to be regarded as legitimate targets by angry or frustrated whites. And, by and large, racial violence was tolerated by the authorities as simply part of the fabric of city life.

It was actually surprising that there wasn't another wave of unrest during the last few years of James Forten's life. Violence peaked at times of economic upheaval, and Philadelphia was mired in a recession, along with the rest of the nation. The Panic of 1837 was rooted in President Andrew Jackson's war against the Philadelphia-based Second Bank of the United States, although admittedly other factors came into play as well. However complex the causes, what businesspeople and ordinary working-people knew was that times were tough.

James Forten ended his long life in business facing a crisis. Shipyards laid off workers, plans for new vessel were scrapped, and shipowners thought twice about which repairs were essential and which could wait until the end of another sailing season. Then there was the credit crunch. Like other investors, James Forten had made loans to people, and they were having trouble paying him back. Businesses that had seemed healthy failed, and once-prosperous merchants defaulted, leaving their creditors with nothing more than a bunch of worthless promissory notes. Like many of his brother merchants, James Forten had to proceed with caution, and like them he lost money. His sons would have to struggle to keep the family business afloat.

Looking back on a lifetime of battles lost and won, how confident could James Forten feel about matters other than business? Had he, for instance, managed to hammer home his message about the American Colonization Society? On one level he could feel fairly sure he had. Few in the Northern free black community supported the ACS, and many of its critics acknowledged the example Forten had set them. White friends in the antislavery movement spoke of his stand against colonization, and some confessed to having been won over from supporting the ACS after talking with him or reading his carefully-reasoned attacks on the society. James Forten knew, though, that the colonization of free black people as far away from the United States as it was possible to ship them was the rallying cry of many whites. Only a minority of them belonged to the ACS, but they shared the society's goals.

Other matters were equally troubling. In the face of legal oppression and mob actions, black leaders in the North seemed unable to agree on an effective course of action. Much of the controversy swirled around the very organization James Forten headed, the American Moral Reform Society. Even if others, some of them old friends, said he and his allies were hopelessly out of touch in insisting that America needed a sweeping moral revolution, he kept the faith—and he would keep it to his dying day. As long as he was able, James Forten spoke at the AMRS's annual conventions, and during his presidency the organization took the radical step of recruiting women as well as men.

There were so many setbacks, though. In the fall of 1839 financial pressures forced the AMRS to stop publishing its monthly journal, the *National Reformer*. The following year the AMRS convention met amid a growing chorus of criticism from within the black community. That criticism grew louder still in 1841. People James Forten liked and respected thought it was time for a new agenda, and critics of the AMRS in Pennsylvania demanded that a state convention be held to thrash out a whole bunch of issues. Things got ugly. A statewide convention was eventually held, but not with James Forten's approval or his participation. The irony was that many of the things the delegates called for—education, the right to vote, economic incentives to improve the lives of people of color—were ones the AMRS had already called for.

Wrangling over ends and means was not confined to black reformers. James Forten was painfully aware of the deep rifts among white abolitionists. There were heated debates over the role of women, the alleged "anti-church" attitude of William Lloyd Garrison and some of those close to him, and a host of other issues. By 1840 organized antislavery had split into two opposing camps—a dismal prospect for those like James Forten, who believed that abolitionists must combine their efforts if they were to have any chance of helping the slaves win their freedom.

It saddened James Forten to differ with friends in the African American leadership in his own city and elsewhere over their agendas. It saddened him to see white friends like Garrison and Arthur Tappan trading insults when both were committed to ending slavery. However, in the last years of his life there were matters much closer to home that saddened him far more. In 1840 his family endured a double tragedy.

On May 11, Gerrit Smith Forten, Robert and Mary's son, died just a few days short of his first birthday. It was only too obvious that Mary would not long survive her child. She was sick with tuberculosis, and in that era, without the benefit of modern drugs, it almost always proved fatal. She passed away just two months after little Gerrit. The deaths of Mary and Gerrit devastated the Forten family. James and Charlotte had known and liked Mary even before Robert began courting her, and they had been overjoyed when the couple married. Her loss, coming on top of the loss of her child, was a blow to the entire family. Robert sold the home they had shared, and he and his young daughter moved in with his parents. He tried to keep busy. He put in long days at the sail-loft. He dusted off the telescope he had made and offered astronomy lessons to the pupils at his friend Daniel Alexander Payne's school. He also continued working with his brother-in-law on the Vigilance Committee, helping to provide food, shelter, money, and safe passage to the hundreds of runaway slaves who showed up in Philadelphia each year.

James and Charlotte grieved for their grandson and their daughter-in-law, and tried to comfort Robert, but they were also growing increasingly worried about another member of the family. Their youngest daughter, Mary Isabella, had always been frail, and now it seemed her health was getting worse. They eventually realized that she, too, had contracted tuberculosis. It could only be a matter of time before they lost her as well.

But if there was sorrow for James and Charotte, there was also joy. They delighted in their children and their grandchildren. By

1840 Harriet and Robert Purvis had presented them with three grandsons and a granddaughter. Robert's daughter, Charlotte, was a great favorite. Sarah and Joseph had two children. And James Jr. and Jane had produced a son and heir, James Vogelsang Forten. Daughter Margaretta remained unmarried, but she had already distinguished herself as a dedicated abolitionist, and she was putting to good use the educational opportunities her parents had been able to give her. Son William, although only in his mid-teens, was obviously bright and able. Thomas might not be as gifted as his siblings, but he was learning the sailmaker's craft and he would always have a job working for his brothers.

With his sons in control of the family business, James Forten retired and settled into the role of elder statesman. Recognition came from many quarters. In 1841 the young men of the Demosthenian Institute, a black literary society, began publishing a newspaper. The feature article each week was "Sketches of Eminent Colored Men in Philadelphia," and the first issue carried an account of the career of "the venerable patriot, James Forten." Famed British novelist and antislavery sympathizer Harriet Martineau, who had visited the Fortens in 1834 on her tour of the United States, sent James Forten a copy of her new novel, *The Hour and the Man,* based on the life of Toussaint Louverture, the hero of the Haitian revolution. The English Quaker Joseph Sturge came to town in the spring of 1841, carrying with him letters of introduction to the leading abolitionists in Philadelphia. He called upon James Forten, whom he described as "an aged and opulent man of colour." Forten's extraordinary life seemed to the Englishman "a practical demonstration of the absurdity...of that prejudice which would stamp the mark of intellectual inferiority on his complexion and race."

Despite his advancing age, James Forten remained devoted to the antislavery cause. Letters from him continued to turn up in abolitionist newspapers, most notably William Lloyd Garrison's *Liberator,* a paper he had supported so generously over the years. As he wrote in the short note Garrison published in the September 17, 1841 issue, "It gives me great pleasure, in reading [the *Liberator*] from week to week, to hear of the…progress of our cause; and I never lay down the *Liberator* without feeling my faith in its final, and I trust speedy triumph, renewed and invigorated."

Zealous abolitionists that they were, James Forten and his family followed with avid interest the fate of the *Amistad* captives. They and their friends saw Joseph Cinqué and the others as courageous freedom-fighters and urged that they be set free by the American courts. Admittedly they had killed several people on the *Amistad,* but they had done so in defense of their liberty. The *Amistad* case became a cause célèbre for the antislavery forces as it worked its way through the courts. Not until 1841 did the United States Supreme Court hand down its ruling that the captives were entitled to their freedom. The Fortens and the Purvises kept themselves informed about every twist and turn in the case. Robert Purvis even commissioned a portrait of Cinqué by Connecticut artist Nathaniel Jocelyn, the brother of abolitionist Simeon S. Jocelyn. He had prints made and donated them to the American Anti-Slavery Society to be sold at a dollar apiece to benefit the organization. Needless to say, James Forten thoroughly approved.

Other matters beside the struggle to end slavery demanded James Forten's attention. In 1840 he did battle with the Philadelphia Board of Education, which was proposing to close the only public high school for black students in the city. *He* could afford to educate his children privately, but he spoke up for the thousands of African American parents who could not.

James Forten had enjoyed good health most of his life, but early in 1841, in his seventy-fifth year, he became seriously ill. His symptoms suggest he was suffering from congestive heart failure. When

Garrison visited him in the spring, he was ailing. As the months went by, he grew worse. He accepted his growing weakness with patience and resignation. He had lived a long life. His family was provided for. He refused to complain. If his illness proved a mortal one, so be it.

By November he was confined to his home. He had made his will several years earlier and saw no reason to change it. Charlotte would have a third of everything he owned. His sister could live in the house he had set aside for her rent-free for the rest of her life. There was a generous bequest to St. Thomas's Church and another to the Philadelphia Anti-Slavery Society. Everything else was to be divided equally among his children.

Ill though he was, James Forten told his family to admit anyone who came to call. Presbyterian minister Stephen H. Gloucester came. Forten spoke kindly of Stephen's late father, John Sr., and said he was glad he had been able to play a part in helping him free his family from slavery. Another visitor was Forten's life-long friend Daniel Brewton. Brewton had never forgotten Forten's selfless act on the *Jersey* sixty years before. Their farewell was a deeply emotional one, and it left Brewton in tears.

African American teacher and preacher Daniel Alexander Payne often spoke with James Forten about his religious faith. Payne reported that Forten told him he was perfectly contented, declaring: "I am ready to leave this world when my Creator calls me." To his own minister, William Douglass, Forten said much the same thing: "The Lord's goodness and mercy have followed me all my days; and the same kind hand is still over me. What He does is right."

James Forten wished to take a final farewell of his family while he still had the strength to speak to them. A few days before he died, he summoned all of them to his bedside. He told his two eldest sons to take care of their mother, and then he turned to Robert Purvis, who had always been like a son to him, and begged him never to forget the plight of the "perishing slaves." James Forten lingered a few more days, and died on the morning of March 4, 1842.

His funeral took place two days later. The procession from his home to St. Thomas's Church was truly remarkable. J. Miller McKim, a white friend from the Pennsylvania Anti-Slavery Society, described it in a letter to the *National Anti-Slavery Standard*. "The vast concourse of people, of all classes and complexions, numbering from three to five thousand, that followed his remains to the grave, bore testimony to the estimation in which he was universally held." Abolitionist Henry C. Wright's report echoed McKim's. "At his funeral, I could but exclaim…HE HAS TRIUMPHED! He gained a victory over a nation arrayed against him: for, around his dead body, *complexion* was forgotten." Those who walked behind James Forten's coffin included "many merchants, shippers, and sea-captains, who had known and respected him for years." Lucretia Mott described it as "a real amalgamation funeral."

That sense of the passing of a unique individual who had, however briefly, bridged the racial divide was evident not only among his fellow abolitionists but among the public in general. The *United States Gazette* described James Forten's funeral as "one of the largest…seen in Philadelphia." White mourners "followed [him] to his grave as a token of their regard for the excellency of his character. He had won the respect of men of all persuasions, and all shades of complexion." The *Public Ledger* observed: "Such a general sinking of respect [as] to color…probably was never before witnessed in this city."

St. Thomas's Church was filled to capacity for the funeral. Rev. Douglass delivered the eulogy. In the seven years Douglass had served at St. Thomas's he had come to know James Forten very well. The older man had befriended him and confided in him. While many self-made men were "mean" and penny-pinching, that could not be said of James Forten. "His heart and hand were ever open to supply the needy," regardless of the color of their skin. It had been his life's work to make his country a better place for all of its citizens. Following the service, James Forten was laid to rest in the small cemetery adjoining the church.

Tributes flowed in from many quarters. From Boston Garrison wrote in praise of his old friend. "He was a man of rare qualities." The editor of the *Herald of Freedom* commented on the attitude of many white Philadelphians with regard to James Forten. "It would have seemed a sort of sacrilege to despise him." The *North American* commented: "His strict integrity and great amenity of manners made him many warm friends among our best citizens." Even the *African Repository*, the official paper of the American Colonization Society, printed a brief memorial, observing that James Forten was "much respected, and justly so" by all classes of society in Philadelphia, even if he was "in error…on the subject of…Colonization."

There was a series of memorial meetings. The first was held the day after the funeral at the First African Presbyterian Church, and Philadelphians attended "without distinction of complexion." James Forten was eulogized as an "honorable patriarch" and a model of "filial and fraternal affection" for his care of his widowed mother and sister. On the evening of March 30, at Mother Bethel, Robert Purvis delivered an address on the life of his father-in-law. A few nights later it was the turn of Stephen H. Gloucester. Even in death James Forten continued to serve the antislavery cause. Copies of Robert Purvis's memorial address were offered for sale at the Anti-Slavery Office in Philadelphia, with the proceeds going to advance the work of abolition.

After the eulogies had been given and the addresses printed and circulated, his fellow citizens continued to speak and write about James Forten's personality, his achievements, and his dedication to the causes he believed in. Perhaps the words that would have pleased him the most were those of an anonymous writer, identified only as a Philadelphia lawyer. The lawyer's final verdict on James Forten was short, simple, and to the point. "He was an honest man."

~

Sweet Freedom's Song

James Forten did not live to see slavery end. He never witnessed the nation he loved torn apart by a bloody civil war, but his children and grandchildren did, and in their different ways they fought to advance what they were sure was the cause of liberty.

James and Charlotte Forten's eldest son, *James Forten Jr.,* and James Jr.'s son, *James Vogelsang Forten,* enlisted in the Union Navy, as did James Forten's sister's son, *James Forten Dunbar.* Another Forten son and two grandsons served in the Union Army. *Joseph Forten Purvis Jr.,* the eldest son of *Sarah Forten* and *Joseph Purvis,* was in several campaigns. One of *Harriet Forten* and *Robert Purvis's* sons, *Charles Burleigh Purvis,* had just finished his medical training in the war's last months—in time to be commissioned as an assistant surgeon to a "colored" regiment. James and Charlotte Forten's second son, the multi-talented *Robert Bridges Forten,* enlisted, rose rapidly through the ranks, and was felled not by an enemy's bullet but by disease. He became the first African American soldier in the history of Philadelphia to be buried with full military honors. Three volleys were fired over his grave in St. Thomas's Churchyard, just feet from where his father lay. On the floor of Congress, Robert's friend, Congressman William D. ("Pig Iron") Kelley, paid tribute to him for his courage and commitment.

It was not only the Forten and Purvis men who helped bring about a Union victory. James and Charlotte Forten's eldest child, *Margaretta Forten*, worked tirelessly on the home front, collecting money and supplies for black soldiers and sailors and the families they left behind. Margaretta's niece, Robert's daughter, *Charlotte L. Forten*, ran many of the same risks as the men in her family. With the war still raging, she traveled to the Sea Islands of South Carolina to teach at a school for ex-slaves.

The struggle for liberty continued once the war was over. The Fortens and the Purvises committed themselves to the campaign for civil rights. *Harriet Forten Purvis* denounced the authorities in Philadelphia for their refusal to let black people ride the city's street cars. Yes, she had a carriage she could use whenever she chose, but she spoke out for the women and men who did not have the advantages she enjoyed.

William Deas Forten, James and Charlotte's youngest child, pushed for the passage of voting rights, and when black men in Pennsylvania finally regained the right they had lost in 1838, he became something of a political power-broker. He and his brother-in-law, *Robert Purvis,* did not always see eye to eye, but they were clear on one thing: without political influence, the African American community would be left in a perilously weak condition. Political power and how it should be used was a reality one of Robert and Harriet Purvis's sons knew a lot about. *Henry Purvis* moved south after the Civil War and served in the South Carolina legislature.

Two of Harriet and Robert's sons entered the medical profession. *Granville Sharp Purvis* trained as a pharmacist and ran a successful business for many years. *Charles Burleigh Purvis* made his home in Washington, D.C. and joined the faculty of Howard University's medical school. He was thrust into the limelight in

1881 when he was the first doctor on the scene when Charles Guiteau shot and fatally wounded President James A. Garfield. Charles could not save the president, but his efforts to do so led to a series of federal appointments.

As a master craftsman himself, James Forten would have been intrigued by the career of another grandson. *William Forten Purvis,* Sarah Forten and Joseph Purvis's son, inherited his grandfather's mechanical skills. Like Thomas Edison, William became a professional inventor. He developed all sorts of mechanical devices and held more than a dozen patents.

Before she married and moved to Kansas, William's sister, *Sarah Forten Purvis,* taught in the public schools in Washington, D.C. Another Forten granddaughter, *Hattie Forten Purvis,* Harriet and Robert Purvis's daughter, devoted her time and energy to the campaign for women's suffrage.

The intertwined Forten and Purvis families endured their share of tragedies. James and Charlotte's youngest daughter, *Mary Isabella,* outlived her father by just a few months. *Harriet* and *Robert Purvis* lost three sons and a daughter. *Sarah Forten Purvis* was widowed young and left to raise eight children on her own. And there was a bitter estrangement between *James Forten Jr.* and most of the rest of the family over his handling of the family business. James Forten's beloved wife, *Charlotte Vandine Forten,* lived through times of profound sadness as well as times of great joy. She died just days short of her one hundredth birthday, a grand lady to the last.

James Forten would have been grieved by some of the members of his family. Their sufferings would have touched him, and a couple would have disappointed him. Overall, though, he would surely have felt intense pride. He had taught them to hold liberty dear and be prepared to fight for it. In their different ways that was a lesson they proved they had learned very well.

Sources and Citations

Introduction – An End and a Beginning

Sir Charles Lyell's eye-witness account of James Forten's funeral appears in his *Travels in North America* (London, 1845), 207.

Chapter 1 – Inheriting Liberty

The best sources on James Forten's family and his childhood are memorial addresses by men who knew him well and talked with him often over the years—Robert Purvis's *Remarks on the Life and Character of James Forten* (Philadelphia, 1842), and Stephen H. Gloucester's *A Discourse Delivered on the Occasion of the Death of Mr. James Forten, Sr.* (Philadelphia, 1843). On slaves and free people of African descent in colonial Pennsylvania, see Gary B. Nash and Jean Soderlund, *Freedom by Degrees* (New York, 1991).

The "tumultuous gatherings" quotation is from "Minutes of the Provincial Council of Pennsylvania," cited in Darold D. Wax, "Africans on the Delaware," *Pennsylvania History* 50 (Jan. 1983), 45. James Forten's statement that "My grandfather obtained his own freedom" is in Samuel J. May's *Some Recollections of Our Anti-Slavery Conflict* (Boston, 1869; reprint. New York, 1968), 287. Ann Elizabeth Forten's will is in the Philadelphia City Archives.

Chapter 2 – Sail-loft and Schoolroom

On the basics of sail-making in the 18th and 19th centuries, see M. F. Brewington, "The Sailmaker's Gear," *American Neptune* 9 (Oct. 1949), and John E. Horsley, *Tools of the Maritime Trades* (Camden, Maine, 1978). The cockroach episode is in James Franklin Briggs, "Sails and Sailmakers," *Old Dartmouth Historical Sketches* 65 (1937). The records of the Friends' African School are in the Friends' Historical Library at Swarthmore College, in Swarthmore, Pennsylvania.

Chapter 3 – Liberty for All?

There are numerous books on African American involvement in the Revolution. See, for example, Benjamin Quarles, *The Negro in the American Revolution* (Chapel Hill, N.C., 1961), Sidney and Emma N. Kaplan, *The Black Pres-*

ence in the Era of the American Revolution (Amherst, Mass., 1989), and Douglas R. Egerton, *Death or Liberty* (New York, 2009).

For an overview of life in Philadelphia before, during and after the British occupation, see John W. Jackson, *With the British Army in Philadelphia* (San Rafael, Calif., 1979). C. Keith Wilbur's *Pirates and Patriots of the Revolution* (Chester, Conn., 1984) is an excellent introduction to the world of the privateers.

James Forten's recollection of hearing the Declaration of Independence read aloud is in *Frederick Douglass' Paper* (Mar. 10, 1848). His statement about the black defenders of Fort Mercer is in a letter he wrote William Lloyd Garrison on Feb. 13, 1831 (Antislavery Manuscripts, Boston Public Library). For the text of Pennsylvania's Gradual Abolition Act, see Roger Bruns, ed., *Am I Not a Man and a Brother?* (New York, 1977), 446-50.

Forten's nagging his mother to let him go to sea, and his mention of the "loud huzzas" when the *Active* was brought into port are in Purvis's *Remarks* (4, 5). Forten described watching the September 2nd parade and seeing black and white soldiers marching side by side in a Feb. 23, 1831 letter to Garrison (Antislavery Manuscripts, BPL).

Chapter 4 – "I Never Will Prove a Traitor"

On the chain of events that led to James Forten's capture, see Harold A. Larrabee, *Decision at the Chesapeake* (New York, 1964). The logs and muster rolls of the *Amphion, La Nymphe,* and *Jersey* are in the Admiralty Records at the National Archives in London.

A number of the men held on board the *Jersey* wrote about their experiences. Thomas Dring's *Recollections of the Jersey Prison-Ship* (Providence, R.I., 1829; reprint. New York, 1961), and Ebenezer Fox's *Adventures* (Boston, 1838) make compelling reading.

Robert Purvis's *Remarks* is the source of the description of Bazely's first taking notice of Forten ("honest and open countenance," 5-6), and Forten's refusal to switch sides ("never will prove a traitor," 6), as well as Forten's allowing Daniel Brewton to escape in his place (7-8), and his memory of his painful trek back to Philadelphia (8). Forten's contrasting of Independence Day celebrations in the 1810s with the situation in 1776 is in his *Letters from a Man of Colour* (Philadelphia, 1813), 7.

Chapter 5 – Venturing to England

Although the log of the *Commerce* has long since disappeared, we can determine from arrival and departure notices in British and American newspapers (*Pennsylvania Packet, New Lloyd's List, London Chronicle*) when James Forten left Philadelphia and how long it took him to cross the Atlantic.

Dorothy Marshall's *Dr. Johnson's London* (New York and London, 1968) is an informative and readable overview of life in the English capital in the 18th century. On black people in Britain at the time of Forten's visit, see Gretchen Gerzina, *Black London: Life Before Emancipation* (New Brunswick, N.J., 1995). In *England, Slaves and Freedom* (Jackson, Miss., 1986) James Walvin gives a clear and concise account of the origins of the British antislavery movement.

Chapter 6 – Mastering His Trade

On sail-making, in addition to the sources listed in **Chap. 1,** see David Steel, *The Art of Sail-Making* (London, 1809), Robert Kipping, *Elementary Treatise on Sails and Sailmaking* 7th ed. (London, 1865), and Emiliano Marino, *The Sailmaker's Apprentice* (Camden, Maine, 1994).

Many of Robert Bridges's business activities are documented in the *Pennsylvania Gazette* (on-line at www.accessiblearchives.com). The deed recording Bridges's purchase of a house for James Forten is in the Philadelphia County Deeds (T. H. Book 179, pp. 244, 248) at the Philadelphia City Archives.

James Forten's rapid rise from apprentice to foreman, and then to junior partner, is described in Purvis, *Remarks* (9), and Gloucester, *A Discourse* (22-23). The story of the patent first appeared in Lydia Maria Child's *The Freedmen's Book* (Boston, 1865). Neither Purvis nor Gloucester mentioned it, and they knew James Forten far better than Child did. (It seems she never met him.) A thorough search of U.S. patent records has failed to reveal any patent held by James Forten or by Robert Bridges.

The statement about tensions with the journeymen, and Bridges's role in winning them over, is in Gloucester, *A Discourse* (23). The importance of Willing & Francis in giving Forten his start in business is noted in the *North American* (Mar. 5, 1842).

Chapter 7 – South Wharves

The relationship between James Forten and Patrick Hayes is detailed in the Barry-Hayes Papers at Philadelphia's Independence Seaport Museum. Forten's ties to members of the Bridges family can be traced through ship registers, city directories, and the files of Philadelphia's leading newspaper for this period, *Poulson's American Daily Advertiser* (on-line at www.genealogybank.com and www.newsbank.com).

Susanna Emlen's comment on Forten's white business associates is in her Dec. 8, 1809 letter to William Dillwyn (Dillwyn Manuscripts, Historical Society of Pennsylvania). Abraham Ritter's observation appears in his *Philadelphia and Her Merchants* (Philadelphia, 1860), 46-47. "Though he belonged to a proscribed race" is from the *National Anti-Slavery Standard* (Mar. 10, 1842).

Sarah Forten told abolitionist Angelina Grimké that several of her father's white workers were employed in the sail-loft the whole of their working lives. Her letter is reprinted in Gilbert H. Barnes and Dwight L. Dumond, eds., *Letters of Theodore Dwight Weld, Angelina Grimké Weld, and Sarah Grimké* (New York, 1934), vol. 1, p. 381.

The story of the river rescues is in Purvis, *Remarks* (11), the *National Anti-Slavery Standard* (Mar. 10, 1842), and Edward S. Abdy, *Journal of a Residence and Tour* (London, 1835; reprint. New York, 1969), vol. 3, pp. 131-32.

The issue of flaxen sailcloth versus cotton canvas is discussed in Alfred W. Crosby Jr., *America, Russia, Hemp, and Napoleon* (Columbus, Ohio, 1965), and Elton W. Hall, "Sailcloth for American Vessels," *American Neptune* 11 (April 1971): 130-45.

Chapter 8 – A Talent for Making Money

Reconstructing James Forten's business activities would have been impossible without the records at the Philadelphia City Archives. Those records include deeds, mortgages, city, county, and state tax ledgers, and the dockets of the Philadelphia District Court and the Court of Common Pleas. Also indispensible for identifying people whose names surface in Forten's business dealings are the United States censuses for 1800-1850 (on-line at www.ancestry.com) and city directories (available in microfiche at various libraries or on-line at www.footnote.com)

A fascinating letter about one loan is Forten to Samuel Breck, July 22, 1828, in the Breck Papers at the Historical Society of Pennsylvania. William Wright's letter to Forten, dated Oct. 12, 1822, is in the Pennsylvania Abolition Society Manuscripts (Loose Correspondence, Incoming, 1820-1849), also at the HSP.

Chapter 9 – Raising a Family in Freedom

Church records provide invaluable information on James Forten's extended family. The Historical Society of Pennsylvania has copies of the registers of Christ Church and Gloria Dei (Old Swedes) Church. The minister, vestry and members of St. Thomas's African Episcopal Church graciously allowed me to consult their registers, which are still housed at the church. Marriage and death announcements appear in *Poulson's American Daily Advertiser*. (See the source notes for **Chap. 7**).

The careers of the members of the Dunbar family who went to sea can be traced in *Maritime Records—Alphabetical—Masters and Crews, 1798-1880*, at the HSP.

The Board of Health Records, which supply data on names, ages, dates of death, causes of death, and places of burial, are at the Philadelphia City Archives. For U.S. census records and Philadelphia city directories, see the source notes for **Chap. 8.**

The manuscript collection of the Pennsylvania Abolition Society is an essential resource for everything from the rescuing of Forten family members from slavery to James Forten's hiring of domestic servants. The original records are at the HSP, but they have been microfilmed, and copies of the microfilm are available at a number of research libraries across the country.

On the school the Fortens and the Douglasses set up, see *Pennsylvania Freeman* (Mar. 17, 1841). The education of the Forten children is detailed in the records of the Clarkson School (Pennsylvania Abolition Society manuscripts), and Samuel J. May, *Some Recollections of Our Anti-Slavery Conflict*, 287-88.

Chapter 10 – A Community Takes Shape

On the situation of Pennsylvania's newly-freed slaves, see Nash and Soderlund, *Freedom By Degrees* (in source notes for **Chap. 1**). The growth of Philadelphia's free black community is discussed in Gary B. Nash, *Forging Freedom* (Cambridge, Mass., 1988), and Julie Winch, *Philadelphia's Black Elite* (Philadelphia, 1988).

The classic work on the yellow fever epidemic is John H. Powell's *Bring Out Your Dead* (Philadelphia, 1949). Although it is a historical novel aimed at a "young adult" audience, readers of all ages will find Laurie Halse Anderson's *Fever 1793* (New York, 2002) engrossing. For the attack on the black community, and the response to it, see Mathew Carey, *A Short Account of the Malignant Fever* (Philadelphia, 1793), and Absalom Jones and Richard Allen, *A Narrative of the Proceedings of the Black People* (Philadelphia, 1794). The 1798 petition is in the *Pennsylvania Gazette* (Feb. 21, 1798).

An essential work on the Free African Society and St. Thomas's Church is William Douglass's *Annals of the First African Church in the United States of America* (Philadelphia, 1862). Douglass reprinted in his book many documents that were subsequently lost or destroyed. St. Thomas's charter is at the Pennsylvania State Archives in Harrisburg (Charters of Incorporation, Book 8, p. 259). See also *Constitution and Rules to be Observed and Kept by the Friendly Society of St. Thomas's Church* (Philadelphia, 1797), in Dorothy B. Porter, ed., *Early Negro Writing* (Boston, 1971).

Although the original has been lost, a microfilmed copy of the Minute Book of Philadelphia's African Lodge can be seen at the library of the Grand Lodge of Massachusetts in Boston. The letters between Prince Hall and the Philadelphians are reprinted in Charles H. Wesley, *Prince Hall, Life and Legacy* (Washington, D.C., 1983).

Chapter 11 – "A Man of Colour" Speaks Out

The full text of the 1799 petition, together with Forten's letter to Thacher, is reprinted in Porter, ed., *Early Negro Writing*, 330-34. On the debate in Congress over the petition, and Thacher's endorsement of it, see Peter M. Bergman and Jean McCarroll, eds., *The Negro in the Congressional Record, 1789-1801* (New York, 1969), 241-44. Forten's letter to the Pennsylvania Abolition Society is in PAS General Meeting Minutes (1800-1824), 26.

The reports of black-on-white violence are from the *Freeman's Journal and Philadelphia Daily Advertiser* (July 7 and July 9, 1804). On the Society for the Suppression of Vice and Immorality, see Douglass, *Annals of the First African Church*, 110-11, 113-14, and William W. Catto, *A Semi-Centenary Discourse* (Philadelphia, 1857), 51. The report of "liberties taken in the public streets" is from *Relf's Gazette* (Nov. 24, 1809).

The celebration of the ending of the slave trade was announced in *Poulson's American Daily Advertiser* (Jan. 1, 1808). Jones's address is reprinted in Porter, ed., *Early Negro Writing*, as are several of the other January 1st orations. For the collection for Captain Hull, see Subscription Lists, 1744-1862, at the Historical Society of Pennsylvania. The comment about using African Americans as cannon-fodder is in the *Democratic Press* (Jan. 13, 1813), cited in Ronald Schultz, *The Republic of Labor* (New York, 1993), 194. A downloadable version of James Forten's *Letters from a Man of Colour* is available in Early American Imprints, Series 2, at www.newsbank.com.

The call for black men to help defend the city is in *Poulson's American Daily Advertiser* (Sept. 19, 1814). Forten's comment about the end of the war is in Forten to Paul Cuffe, Feb. 15, 1815, Cuffe Papers, New Bedford Free Public Library, New Bedford, Mass.

Chapter 12 – Captain Cuffe's Plan

Lamont D. Thomas's *Rise to be a People* (Urbana, Ill., 1986), and Rosalind Cobb Wiggins's *Captain Paul Cuffe's Logs and Letters* (Washington, D.C., 1996) are superbly researched accounts of Cuffe's life and work. His manuscripts are housed in two locations in New Bedford—the Free Public Library (Cuffe Papers – CP) and the Old Dartmouth Historical Society Library (Cuffe Letters – CL).

On the idea of building a ship to trade with Africa, see Cuffe to Forten, Jan. 27, 1815 (CL), and Forten to Cuffe, Feb. 15, 1815 (CP). For Cuffe's opinion of Antoine Servance, see Cuffe to William Allen, Apr. 1, 1816 (CP). Forten's approach to the African Institution is detailed in Forten to Cuffe, Oct. 10, 1815 (CL), and Forten and Parrott to the Directors of the African Institution, Nov. 15, 1815, in African Institution, *Tenth Report* (London, 1816), 70-71.

Cuffe's growing interest in a settlement plan can be seen in Mills to Cuffe, July 10, 1815 (CP), and Cuffe to Mills, Aug. 6, 1815 (CP). Cuffe's request that Forten recruit craftsmen is in Cuffe to Forten, Aug. 14, 1816 (CP). For Cuffe's contact with Robert Finley, see Finley to Cuffe, Dec. 6, 1816 (CP), and Cuffe to Finley, Jan. 8, 1817 (CP). Cuffe wrote of the need to involve black people in the planning of a colony in his letter to Mills on Jan. 6, 1817 (CP). Forten's statement that "the People of Colour here was very much fri[gh]tened" is in Forten to Cuffe, Jan. 25, 1817 (CP).

The sense of the Bethel meeting is clearly seen in *Resolutions and Remonstrances of the People of Colour Against Colonization* (Philadelphia, 1818). Finley's discussions with the Philadelphians are described in Isaac V. Brown, *Biography of the Rev. Robert Finley* (Philadelphia, 1857; reprint. New York, 1969), 2nd ed., 122-24. Forten's "become a people" comment is in his Jan. 25, 1817 letter to Cuffe (CP).

On the American Colonization Society, see P. J. Staudenraus, *The African Colonization Movement* (New York, 1961), and Eric Burin, *Slavery and the Peculiar Solution* (Gainesville, Fla., 2005). The huge collection of ACS papers in the Library of Congress is searchable on-line at www.footnote.com.

Chapter 13 — "America Is Our True Home"

"A Merchant I work for" is in Forten to Cuffe, Apr. 14, 1817 (CP). Forten's insistence that there must be a colony is in his July 25, 1817 letter to Cuffe (CP). On white support for colonization in Philadelphia in the summer of 1817, see *Poulson's American Daily Advertiser,* Aug. 8, Aug. 9 and Aug. 12, 1817. For the August 10 protest, see "Address of the free people of colour," in *Minutes of a Special Meeting of the Fifteenth American Convention, for Promoting the Abolition of Slavery* (Philadelphia, 1818), i-iv.

Word of Cuffe's death came in Rhoda Cuffe to Forten, Sept. 10, 1817 (CP). For the November 1819 protest, see *Niles' Register* (Nov. 27, 1819). Forten's "Man of Colour" letter was published in the *Union United States Gazette* (Dec. 11, 1819). "The ideas of Cornish & Forten" is in William B. Davidson to R. R. Gurley, Feb. 16, 1827 (ACS Papers). For statements by Forten (writing under his pen-name, "A Man of Colour"), see *Freedom's Journal* (May 18 and June 8, 1827). Russwurm announced his support of colonization in an editorial in *Freedom's Journal* on February 14, 1829.

Chapter 14 – Allies in Liberty's Cause

An excellent account of William Lloyd Garrison's life is Henry Mayer's *All on Fire* (New York, 1998). Most of James Forten's letters to Garrison are in the Antislavery Manuscripts in the Boston Public Library.

Essential resources for exploring the antislavery movement are the various antislavery newspapers, some of which are available on-line, and the personal papers of people involved in the movement. The Black Abolitionist

Papers microfilm (Ann Arbor, Mich., 1981-83) is invaluable, but if working through seventeen rolls of microfilm proves too daunting, the five-volume *Black Abolitionist Papers,* edited by C. Peter Ripley (Chapel Hill, N.C., 1989-91) is very accessible and well-indexed.

For "We are acquainted with the writer," see Forten to Garrison, Dec. 31, 1830, and *Liberator* (Jan. 8, 1831); "bail out the Delaware" is in the *Liberator* (Jan. 22, 1831); "as good citizens as the whites" is also in the *Liberator* (Feb. 12, 1831). "Men Must Be Free" appeared in the *Liberator* on Aug. 20, 1831. For "Indeed we live in stirring times," see Forten to Garrison, Oct. 20, 1831.

On the New Haven manual labor college, see *College for Colored Youth* (New York, 1831), and Forten to Garrison, Oct. 20, 1831. The story of Prudence Crandall's ill-fated school is told in Susan Strane's *A Whole-Souled Woman* (New York, 1990). Forten's endorsement of the school appeared in the *Liberator* (Mar. 9, 1833).

For Forten's criticism of the ACS, see his Feb. 23 and Oct. 20, 1831 letters to Garrison, and his letter (signed "F") to *Poulson's American Daily Advertiser* (Oct. 26, 1831). The controversy that arose in Philadelphia in the summer of 1833 is described in the *Emancipator* (July 13 and July 20, 1833).

Forten wrote Garrison on May 6 and July 28, 1832 enthusiastically endorsing his *Thoughts on African Colonization.* The pamphlet's impact on one of the ACS's major supporters is recounted in Lewis Tappan's *The Life of Arthur Tappan* (New York, 1871; reprint. Westport, Conn., 1970), 136-37. Forten's "even then, at the very onset" comment is in the *Liberator* (Aug. 1, 1835).

On the founding of the American Anti-Slavery Society, see *Liberator* (Dec. 14, 1833). The annual reports of the AASS provide information on the involvement of the Forten family. The records of the Philadelphia Female Anti-Slavery Society, the Philadelphia Anti-Slavery Society, and the Young Men's Anti-Slavery Society of Philadelphia have been microfilmed as part of the Pennsylvania Abolition Society Manuscripts collection. On the role of James Forten and his extended family in founding the Pennsylvania Anti-Slavery Society, see *Proceedings of the Pennsylvania Convention, Assembled to Organize a State Anti-Slavery Society* (Philadelphia, 1837).

Chapter 15 – A Family Commitment

The Fortens' speeches and writings were often published in the *Liberator.* Generally they identified themselves, but Sarah used two pen-names, "Ada" and "Magawisca." On Robert Purvis's trip to Britain, see Daniel Alexander Payne's *Recollections of Seventy Years* (Nashville, 1888; reprint. New York, 1968), 53-54, and *Anti-Slavery Record,* Nov. 1835 (Appendix).

"The Grave of the Slave" is in the Jan. 22, 1831 issue of the *Liberator.* For the musical setting, see Charles K. Jones and Lorenzo K. Greenwich, comps., *A Choice Collection of the Works of Francis Johnson* (New York, 1987), vol. 2, pp. 200-201. Garrison learned "Ada's" identity in James Forten to Garrison, Feb. 23, 1831. Sarah's letter to Angelina Grimké is in Barnes and Dumond, eds., *Weld-Grimké Letters,* vol. 1, pp. 379-81.

James Forten Jr's letter, signed "F," is in the Mar. 19, 1831 issue of the *Liberator.* His identity is revealed in James Forten to Garrison, Mar. 21, 1831. The charter he helped write for the Library Company of Colored Persons is in Charters of Incorporation, Book 6, p. 54, in the Pennsylvania State Archives in Harrisburg.

On Robert B. Forten's intellectual abilities, see Payne, *Recollections,* 51-52. On William's time at Oneida, and his father's support of the school, see Milton C. Sernett, *Abolition's Axe* (Syracuse, N.Y., 1986), 41, 53-54, 58, and *Pennsylvania Freeman,* July 25, 1839.

For the various wedding announcements, see *Poulson's American Daily Advertiser,* Sept. 16, 1831 (Harriet Forten and Robert Purvis); *Public Ledger,* Jan. 12, 1838 (Sarah Forten and Joseph Purvis); *Public Ledger,* Oct. 21, 1836 (Robert B. Forten and Mary Wood); and *New York Herald,* Jan. 15, 1839 (James Forten Jr. and Jane Vogelsang).

It was the custom in 19th-century America for genteel young ladies to have albums in which family and friends would write poetry and prose, paint pictures, or do pieces of calligraphy. Mary Wood's album has survived, and is housed, along with that of Elizabeth Smith, in Howard University's Moorland-Spingarn Research Center. Three more albums belonging to sisters Martina and Mary Ann Dickerson and to Amy M. Cassey can be found at the Library Company of Philadelphia. All five contain work by members of the Forten family.

Robert Purvis and his in-laws were involved in helping runaway slaves. Their activities can be traced through the minute book of the Philadelphia Vigilance Committee, which is preserved in the Historical Society of Pennsylvania's Leon Gardiner Collection.

Chapter 16 – Law-Breakers and Lawmakers

The meeting in the tavern is reported in *United States Gazette* (Nov. 30, 1831). On the response of Forten and his friends, see James Forten, Robert Purvis, and William Whipper, *To the Honorable the Senate of Pennsylvania* (Philadelphia, 1832).

By far the best sources on the race riots—although admittedly they are not unbiased—are the Philadelphia newspapers of the period. Many of them are searchable on-line at www.genealogybank.com or www.newsbank.com. On the 1834 riot, see Edward S. Abdy, *Journal of a Residence and Tour,* vol. 3, p. 319. That riot and the unrest that broke out the following year are described in vivid detail in *Hazard's Register* (Aug. 23, 1834 and July 18, 1835).

Andrew Bell was the Englishman who asked the naïve question about black voting rights. See his *Men and Things in America* (London, 1838), 179. Samuel Breck noted his exchange with Forten. Nicholas B. Wainwright, ed., "The Diary of Samuel Breck, 1814-1822," *Pennsylvania Magazine of History and Biography* 102 (Oct. 1978), 505. The cropping up of Forten's name in the debates over the voting rights issue can be traced in the *Proceedings and Debates of the Convention of the Commonwealth of Pennsylvania* (Harrisburg, 1837-39). See especially vol. 3, pp. 82-83, 85, and vol. 10, pp. 112, 126-27.

On the bid to prevent ratification, see Robert Purvis et al., *Appeal of Forty Thousand Citizens* (Philadelphia, 1838). John Joseph Gurney noted (102) the exchange between the two children in the street in *A Visit to North America* (Norwich, England, 1841). The "departed liberty" quotation is from the *Provincial Freeman* (Aug. 15, 1857), www.accessiblearchives.com.

Chapter 17 – Keeping Hope Alive

On the 1838 riot, see *History of Pennsylvania Hall, Which was Destroyed by a Mob on the 17th of May, 1838* (Philadelphia, 1838; reprint. New York, 1969).

For a discussion of the American Moral Reform Society during its brief but tension-filled existence, see Julie Winch, *Philadelphia's Black Elite*

(Philadelphia, 1988). For examples of the criticism leveled against the organization, see *Colored American* (Aug. 26 and Sept. 2, 1837) at www.accessiblearchives.com

Chapter 18 – An Honest Man

In *The Condition, Elevation, Emigration and Destiny of the Colored People* (Philadelphia, 1852; reprint. New York, 1968) Martin R. Delany describes (94) one business failure that affected James Forten. The inventory of Forten's estate—his will is in the Philadelphia City Archives—reveals many loans classed as "doubtful." In other words, the borrowers could not pay up.

The American Moral Reform Society's annual meetings are covered in detail in the *Colored American* and the *Liberator,* as is the discussion over holding a state convention.

There is a long obituary of Mary Wood Forten in the *Colored American* (Aug. 29, 1840). The sketch of James Forten in the *Demosthenian Shield* was reprinted in the *Colored American* (July 24, 1841). Harriet Martineau described her visit with James Forten in a letter to his granddaughter, Charlotte. See Anna Julia Cooper, ed., *Personal Recollections of the Grimké Family* (Washington, D.C., 1951), 39. Joseph Sturge recounted his meeting with Forten in *A Visit to the United States in 1841* (London, 1842; reprint. New York, 1969), 10.

On the Cinqué painting, see *National Anti-Slavery Standard* (Feb. 25, 1841). The context of Forten's battle with the Board of Education is explained in Harry C. Silcox, "Delay and Neglect: Negro Education in Antebellum Phila-delphia," *Pennsylvania Magazine of History and Biography* 97 (Oct. 1978): 444-64.

Robert Purvis described Daniel Brewton's last meeting with James Forten in his *Remarks,* 8. Forten's conversations with Payne and Douglass, and his part-ing words to his family, are in the *Liberator* (Mar. 18, 1842). McKim's ac-count of the funeral is in the *National Anti-Slavery Standard* (Mar. 17, 1842). Wright's report is in the *Liberator.* (Mar. 18, 1842), and Mott's is in Lucretia Mott to Richard and Hannah Webb, Mar. 7, 1842, in Anna Davis Hallowell, ed., *James and Lucretia Mott, Life and Letters* (Boston, 1884), 232. The re-ports from the *United States Gazette* and the *Public Ledger* were reprinted in the *Liberator* (Mar. 11 and Mar. 18, 1842). Douglass's eulogy is in the *Libera-tor* (May 5, 1842). Garrison's March 18, 1842 letter to Sarah M. Douglass is in the Antislavery Manuscripts at the Boston Public Library.

For other tributes see *Herald of Freedom* (Mar. 1, 1842), *North American* (Mar. 5, 1842), and *African Repository* 18 (May 1842). The memorial meetings, and the sale of Purvis's *Remarks* as an antislavery fund-raiser, are in the *National Anti-Slavery Standard* (Mar. 24, 1842), and *Pennsylvania Freeman* (April 1842). "He was an honest man" appears in *Wealth and Biography of the Wealthy Citizens of Philadelphia, By a Member of the Philadelphia Bar* (Philadelphia, 1845), 10.

Selected Resources

Websites

www.accessiblearchives.com
www.ancestry.com
www.footnote.com
www.genealogybank.com
www.newsbank.com

Libraries and Archives

Boston Public Library (Department of Rare Books and Manuscripts)
Friends' Historical Library, Swarthmore College
Historical Society of Pennsylvania, Philadelphia
Independence Seaport, Philadelphia
Library Company of Philadelphia
Moorland-Spingarn Research Center, Howard University
New Bedford Free Public Library, New Bedford, Mass.
Old Dartmouth Historical Society Library, New Bedford, Mass.
Pennsylvania State Archives, Harrisburg
Philadelphia City Archives

Books and Articles

Abdy, Edward S. *Journal of a Residence and Tour.* London: John Murray, 1835; reprint. New York: Negro Universities Press, 1969.

Brown, Isaac V. *Biography of the Rev. Robert Finley.* Philadelphia, 1857; reprint. New York: Arno, 1969

Catto, William W. *A Semi-Centenary Discourse.* Philadelphia: Joseph M. Wilson, 1857.

Douglass, William. *Annals of the First African Church in the United States of America.* Philadelphia: King and Baird, 1862.

Forten, James, *Letters from a Man of Colour on a Late Bill Before the Senate of Pennsylvania.* Philadelphia, 1813.

Forten, James, Robert Purvis, and William Whipper, *To the Honorable the Senate of Pennsylvania.* Philadelphia, 1832.

Gloucester, Stephen H. *A Discourse Delivered on the Occasion of the Death of Mr. James Forten, Sr.* Philadelphia: I. Ashmead, 1843.

May, Samuel J. *Some Recollections of Our Anti-Slavery Conflict.* Boston: Fields, Osgood, 1869; reprint. New York: Arno, 1968.

Mayer, Henry. *All on Fire.* New York: St. Martin's Press, 1998.

Nash, Gary B. *Forging Freedom.* Cambridge, Mass.: Harvard University Press, 1988.

_____ and Jean Soderlund. *Freedom by Degrees.* New York: Oxford University Press, 1991.

Payne, Daniel Alexander. *Recollections of Seventy Years.* Nashville: AME Sunday School Union, 1888; reprint. New York: Arno, 1968.

Porter, Dorothy B., ed. *Early Negro Writing.* Boston: Beacon Press, 1971.

Purvis, Robert. *Remarks on the Life and Character of James Forten.* Philadelphia: Merrihew and Thompson, 1842.

Resolutions and Remonstrances of the People of Colour Against Colonization on the Coast of Africa. Philadelphia, 1818.

Ripley, C. Peter, ed. *Black Abolitionist Papers.* Chapel Hill, N.C.: University of North Carolina Press, 1989-91. (5 vols.)

Ritter, Abraham. *Philadelphia and Her Merchants.* Philadelphia: The Author, 1860.

Thomas, Lamont D. *Rise to be a People.* Urbana, Ill.: University of Illinois Press, 1986

Wiggins, Rosalind Cobb. *Captain Paul Cuffe's Logs and Letters.* Washington, D.C.: Howard University Press, 1996.

Winch, Julie. *Philadelphia's Black Elite.* Philadelphia: Temple University Press, 1988.